STUDY NOTES

CURRENT AFFAIRS February 2023

CONTENT TABLE

CURRENT AFFAIRS FEBRUARY 2023

TOPICS	PAGE NO
The Union Budget 2023-24	04 - 17
Grammy Awards 2023 Winners List	17 - 18
A "Golden Book Awards" 2023 Announced	18 - 21
RBI Monetary Policy February 2023	21 - 22
World Happiness Index 2023	22 - 23
President Draupadi Murmu named new governors in 12 states and 1UT	24 - 25
Shuman Gill and Grace Scrivens named ICC Men's and Women's Play-er of January	25 - 26
5th Khelo India Youth Games 2022	26 - 29
Dadasaheb Phalke International Film Festival Awards 2023	29 - 31
Sansad Ratna award 2023	31 - 32
ICC Women's T20 World Cup 2023	32 - 33
Banking and Financial Current Affairs	33 - 39
Economy Current Affairs	39 - 41
Business Current Affairs	41 - 45

International Current Affairs	45 - 53
National Current Affairs	53 - 59
States Current Affairs	59 - 64
Schemes/Committees	64 - 69
Appointments/Resignations (National & International)	69 - 72
Ranks and Reports	72 - 74
Sports Current Affairs	74 - 79
Summits And Conferences	79 - 81
Awards & Recognition	81 - 84
Important Days	84 - 88
Defence Current Affairs	88 - 91
Science and Technology	91 - 95
Books & Authors	95 - 96
Miscellaneous Current Affairs	96 - 100
Obituaries	100 - 103

FEBRUARY 2023
CURRENT AFFAIRS

The union budget 2023-24

The Union Minister of Finance and Corporate Affairs Smt. Nirmala Sitharaman presented the Union Budget 2023-24 in Parliament. The highlights of the Budget are as follows:

- Per capita income has more than doubled to ₹1.97 lakh in around nine years.
- Indian economy has increased in size from being 10th to 5th largest in the world in the past nine years.
- EPFO membership has more than doubled to 27 crore.
- 7,400 crore digital payments of ₹126 lakh crore has taken place through UPI in 2022.
- 11.7 crore household toilets constructed under Swachh Bharat Mission.
- 9.6 crore LPG connections provided under Ujjwala.
- 220 crore covid vaccination of 102 crore persons.
- 47.8 crore PM Jan Dhan bank accounts.
- Insurance cover for 44.6 crore persons under PM Suraksha Bima and PM Jeevan Jyoti Yojana.
- Cash transfer of ₹2.2 lakh crore to over 11.4 crore farmers under PM Kisan Samman Nidhi.
- Seven priorities of the budget 'Saptarishi' are inclusive development, reaching the last mile, infrastructure and investment, unleashing the potential, green growth, youth power and financial sector.
- Atmanirbhar Clean Plant Program with an outlay of ₹2200 crore to be launched to boost availability of disease-free, quality planting material for high value horticultural crops.
- 157 new nursing colleges to be established in co-location with the existing 157 medical colleges established since 2014.

- Centre to recruit 38,800 teachers and support staff for the 740 Eklavya Model Residential Schools, serving 3.5 lakh tribal students over the next three years.
- Outlay for PM Awas Yojana is being enhanced by 66% to over Rs. 79,000 crore.
- Capital outlay of Rs. 2.40 lakh crore has been provided for the Railways, which is the highest ever outlay and about nine times the outlay made in 2013-14.
- Urban Infrastructure Development Fund (UIDF) will be established through use of priority Sector Lending shortfall, which will be managed by the national Housing Bank, and will be used by public agencies to create urban infrastructure in Tier 2 and Tier 3 cities.
- Entity DigiLocker to be setup for use by MSMEs, large business and charitable trusts to store and share documents online securely.
- 100 labs to be setup for 5G services based application development to realize a new range of opportunities, business models, and employment potential.
- 500 new 'waste to wealth' plants under GOBARdhan (Galvanizing Organic Bio-Agro Resources Dhan) scheme to be established for promoting circular economy at total investment of Rs 10,000 crore. 5 per cent compressed biogas mandate to be introduced for all organizations marketing natural and bio gas.
- Centre to facilitate one crore farmers to adopt natural farming over the next three years. For this, 10,000 BioInput Resource Centres to be set-up, creating a national-level distributed micro-fertilizer and pesticide manufacturing network.
- Pradhan Mantri Kaushal Vikas Yojana 4.0, to be launched to skill lakhs of youth within the next three years covering new age courses for Industry 4.0 like coding, AI, robotics, mechatronics, IOT, 3D printing, drones, and soft skills.
- 30 Skill India International Centres to be set up across different States to skill youth for international opportunities.
- Revamped credit guarantee scheme for MSMEs to take effect from 1st April 2023 through infusion of Rs 9,000 crore in the corpus. This scheme would enable additional collateral-free guaranteed credit of Rs 2 lakh crore and also reduce the cost of the credit by about 1 per cent.

- Central Processing Centre to be setup for faster response to companies through centralized handling of various forms filed with field offices under the Companies Act.
- The maximum deposit limit for Senior Citizen Savings Scheme to be enhanced from Rs 15 lakh to Rs 30 lakh.
- Targeted Fiscal Deficit to be below 4.5% by 2025-26.
- Agriculture Accelerator Fund to be set-up to encourage agri-startups by young entrepreneurs in rural areas.
- To make India a global hub for 'Shree Anna', the Indian Institute of Millet Research, Hyderabad will be supported as the Centre of Excellence for sharing best practices, research and technologies at the international level.
- ₹20 lakh crore agricultural credit targeted at animal husbandry, dairy and fisheries.
- A new sub-scheme of PM Matsya Sampada Yojana with targeted investment of ₹6,000 crore to be launched to further enable activities of fishermen, fish vendors, and micro & small enterprises, improve value chain efficiencies, and expand the market. Digital public infrastructure for agriculture to be built as an open source, open standard and inter operable public good to enable inclusive farmer centric solutions and support for growth of agri-tech industry and start-ups.
- Computerisation of 63,000 Primary Agricultural Credit Societies (PACS) with an investment of ₹2,516 crore initiated.
- Massive decentralised storage capacity to be set up to help farmers store their produce and realize remunerative prices through sale at appropriate times.
- Sickle Cell Anaemia elimination mission to be launched.
- Joint public and Private Medical research to be encouraged via select ICMR labs for encouraging collaborative research and innovation.
- New Programme to promote research in Pharmaceuticals to be launched.

- Rs. 10 lakh crore capital investment, a steep increase of 33% for third year in a row, to enhance growth potential and job creation, crowd-in private investments, and provide a cushion against global headwinds.
- Aspirational Blocks Programme covering 500 blocks launched for saturation of essential government services across multiple domains such as health, nutrition, education, agriculture, water resources, financial inclusion, skill development, and basic infrastructure.
- Rs. 15,000 crore for implementation of Pradhan Mantri PVTG Development Mission over the next three years under the Development Action Plan for the Scheduled Tribes.
- Investment of Rs. 75,000 crore, including Rs. 15,000 crore from private sources, for one hundred critical transport infrastructure projects, for last and first mile connectivity for ports, coal, steel, fertilizer, and food grains sectors.
- New Infrastructure Finance Secretariat established to enhance opportunities for private investment in infrastructure.
- District Institutes of Education and Training to be developed as vibrant institutes of excellence for Teachers' Training.
- A National Digital Library for Children and Adolescents to be set-up for facilitating availability of quality books across geographies, languages, genres and levels, and device agnostic accessibility.
- Rs. 5,300 crore to be given as central assistance to Upper Bhadra Project to provide sustainable micro irrigation and filling up of surface tanks for drinking water.
- 'Bharat Shared Repository of Inscriptions' to be set up in a digital epigraphy museum, with digitization of one lakh ancient inscriptions in the first stage.
- 'Effective Capital Expenditure' of Centre to be Rs. 13.7 lakh crore. - Continuation of 50-year interest free loan to state governments for one more year to spur investment in infrastructure and to incentivize them for complementary policy actions.
- Encouragement to states and cities to undertake urban planning reforms and actions to transform our cities into 'sustainable cities of tomorrow'.

- Transition from manhole to machine-hole mode by enabling all cities and towns to undertake 100 percent mechanical desludging of septic tanks and sewers.
- IGOT Karmayogi, an integrated online training platform, launched to provide continuous learning opportunities for lakhs of government employees to upgrade their skills and facilitate people-centric approach.
- More than 39,000 compliances reduced and more than 3,400 legal provisions decriminalized to enhance Ease Of Doing Business.
- Jan Vishwas Bill to amend 42 Central Acts have been introduced to further trust-based governance.
- Three centres of excellence for Artificial Intelligence to be set-up in top educational institutions to realise the vision of "Make AI in India and Make AI work for India".
- National Data Governance Policy to be brought out to unleash innovation and research by start-ups and academia.
- One stop solution for reconciliation and updation of identity and address of individuals to be established using DigiLocker service and Aadhaar as foundational identity.
- PAN will be used as the common identifier for all digital systems of specified government agencies to bring in Ease of Doing Business.
- 95 per cent of the forfeited amount relating to bid or performance security, will be returned to MSME's by government and government undertakings in cases the MSME's failed to execute contracts during Covid period.
- Result Based Financing to better allocate scarce resources for competing development needs.
- Phase-3 of the E-Courts project to be launched with an outlay of Rs. 7,000 crore for efficient administration of justice.
- R & D grant for Lab Grown Diamonds (LGD) sector to encourage indigenous production of LGD seeds and machines and to reduce import dependency.

- Annual production of 5 MMT under Green Hydrogen Mission to be targeted by 2030 to facilitate transition of the economy to low carbon intensity and to reduce dependence on fossil fuel imports.
- ₹35000 crore outlay for energy security, energy transition and net zero objectives.
- Battery energy storage systems to be promoted to steer the economy on the sustainable development path.
- 20,700 crore outlay provided for renewable energy grid integration and evacuation from Ladakh.
- "PM Programme for Restoration, Awareness, Nourishment and Amelioration of Mother Earth" (PM-PRANAM) to be launched to incentivize States and Union Territories to promote alternative fertilizers and balanced use of chemical fertilizers.
- 'Mangrove Initiative for Shoreline Habitats & Tangible Incomes', MISHTI, to be taken up for mangrove plantation along the coastline and on salt pan lands, through convergence between MGNREGS, CAMPA Fund and other sources.
- Green Credit Programme to be notified under the Environment (Protection) Act to incentivize and mobilize additional resources for environmentally sustainable and responsive actions.
- Amrit Dharohar scheme to be implemented over the next three years to encourage optimal use of wetlands, enhance bio-diversity, carbon stock, eco-tourism opportunities and income generation for local communities.
- A unified Skill India Digital platform to be launched for enabling demand-based formal skilling, linking with employers including MSMEs, and facilitating access to entrepreneurship schemes.
- Direct Benefit Transfer under a pan-India National Apprenticeship Promotion Scheme to be rolled out to provide stipend support to 47 lakh youth in three years.
- At least 50 tourist destinations to be selected through challenge mode; to be developed as a complete package for domestic and foreign tourists.

- Sector specific skilling and entrepreneurship development to be dovetailed to achieve the objectives of the 'Dekho Apna Desh' initiative.

- Tourism infrastructure and amenities to be facilitated in border villages through the Vibrant Villages Programme.

- States to be encouraged to set up a Unity Mall for promotion and sale of their own and also all others states' ODOPs (One District, One Product), GI products and handicrafts.

- National Financial Information Registry to be set up to serve as the central repository of financial and ancillary information for facilitating efficient flow of credit, promoting financial inclusion, and fostering financial stability. A new legislative framework to be designed in consultation with RBI to govern this credit public infrastructure.

- Financial sector regulators to carry out a comprehensive review of existing regulations in consultation with public and regulated entities. Time limits to decide the applications under various regulations would also be laid down.

- To enhance business activities in GIFT IFSC, the following measures to be taken.

- Delegating powers under the SEZ Act to IFSCA to avoid dual regulation. - Setting up a single window IT system for registration and approval from IFSCA, SEZ authorities, GSTN, RBI, SEBI and IRDAI.

- Permitting acquisition financing by IFSC Banking Units of foreign bank.

- Establishing a subsidiary of EXIM Bank for trade refinancing.

- Amending IFSCA Act for statutory provisions for arbitration, ancillary services, and avoiding dual regulation under SEZ Act.

- Recognizing offshore derivative instruments as valid contracts.

- Amendments proposed to the Banking Regulation Act, the Banking Companies Act and the Reserve of India Act to improve bank governance and enhance investors protection.

- Countries looking for digital continuity solutions would be facilitated for setting up of their Data Embassies in GIFT IFSC.
- SEBI to be empowered to develop, regulate, maintain and enforce norms and standards for education in the National Institute of Securities Markets and to recognize award of degrees, diplomas and certificates.
- Integrated IT portal to be established to enable investors to easily reclaim the unclaimed shares and unpaid dividends from the Investor Education and Protection Fund Authority.
- To commemorate Azadi Ka Amrit Mahotsav, a one-time new small savings scheme, Mahila Samman Savings Certificate to be launched. It will offer deposit facility upto Rs 2 lakh in the name of women or girls for tenure of 2 years (up to March 2025) at fixed interest rate of 7.5 per cent with partial withdrawal option.
- The maximum deposit limit for Monthly Income Account Scheme to be enhanced from Rs 4.5 lakh to Rs 9 lakh for single account and from Rs 9 lakh to Rs 15 lakh for joint account.
- The entire fifty-year interest free loan to states to be spent on capital expenditure within 2023-24. Part of the loan is conditional on States increasing actual Capital expenditure and parts of outlay will be linked to States undertaking specific loans.
- Fiscal Deficit of 3.5% of GSDP allowed for States of which 0.5% is tied to Power sector reforms.

Revised Estimates 2022-23

- The total receipts other than borrowings is Rs 24.3 lakh crore, of which the net tax receipts are Rs 20.9 lakh crore.
- The total expenditure is Rs 41.9 lakh crore, of which the capital expenditure is about Rs 7.3 lakh crore.
- The fiscal deficit is 6.4 per cent of GDP, adhering to the Budget Estimate.

Budget Estimates 2023-24

- The total receipts other than borrowings are estimated at Rs 27.2 lakh crore and the total expenditure is estimated at Rs 45 lakh crore.
- The net tax receipts are estimated at Rs 23.3 lakh crore.
- The fiscal deficit is estimated to be 5.9 per cent of GDP.
- To finance the fiscal deficit in 2023-24, the net market borrowings from dated securities are estimated at Rs 11.8 lakh crore.
- The gross market borrowings are estimated at Rs 15.4 lakh crore.

Direct Taxes

- Direct Tax proposals aim to maintain continuity and stability of taxation, further simplify and rationalise various provisions to reduce the compliance burden, promote the entrepreneurial spirit and provide tax relief to citizens.

- Constant endeavour of the Income Tax Department to improve Tax Payers Services by making compliance easy and smooth.

- To further improve tax payer services, proposal to roll out a next-generation Common IT Return Form for tax payer convenience, along with plans to strengthen the grievance redressal mechanism.

- Rebate limit of Personal Income Tax to be increased to Rs. 7 lakh from the current Rs. 5 lakh in the new tax regime. Thus, persons in the new tax regime, with income up to Rs. 7 lakh to not pay any tax.

- Tax structure in new personal income tax regime, introduced in 2020 with six income slabs, to change by reducing the number of slabs to five and increasing the tax exemption limit to Rs. 3 lakh. Change to provide major relief to all tax payers in the new regime.

Total Income (Rs)	**Rate (per cent)**
Up to 3,00,000	Nil
From 3,00,001 to 6,00,000	5
From 6,00,001 to 9,00,000	10
From 9,00,001 to 12,00,000	15

From 12,00,001 to 15,00,000	20
Above 15,00,000	30

- Proposal to extend the benefit of standard deduction of Rs. 50,000 to salaried individual, and deduction from family pension up to Rs. 15,000, in the new tax regime.
- Highest surcharge rate to reduce from 37 per cent to 25 per cent in the new tax regime. This too further result in reduction of the maximum personal income tax rate to 39 per cent.
- The limit for tax exemption on leave encashment on retirement of non-government salaried employees to increase to Rs. 25 lakh.
- The new income tax regime to be made the default tax regime. However, citizens will continue to have the option to avail the benefit of the old tax regime.
- Enhanced limits for micro enterprises and certain professionals for availing the benefit of presumptive taxation proposed. Increased limit to apply only in case the amount or aggregate of the amounts received during the year, in cash, does not exceed five per cent of the total gross receipts/turnover.
- Deduction for expenditure incurred on payments made to MSMEs to be allowed only when payment is actually made in order to support MSMEs in timely receipt of payments.
- New co-operatives that commence manufacturing activities till 31.3.2024 to get the benefit of a lower tax rate of 15 per cent, as presently available to new manufacturing companies.
- Opportunity provided to sugar co-operatives to claim payments made to sugarcane farmers for the period prior to assessment year 2016-17 as expenditure. This expected to provide them a relief of almost Rs. 10,000 crore.
- Provision of a higher limit of Rs. 2 lakh per member for cash deposits to and loans in cash by Primary Agricultural Co-operative Societies (PACS) and Primary Co-operative Agriculture and Rural Development Banks (PCARDBs).

- A higher limit of Rs. 3 crore for TDS on cash withdrawal to be provided to co-operative societies.
- Date of incorporation for income tax benefits to startups to be extended from 31.03.23 to 31.3.24.
- Proposal to provide the benefit of carry forward of losses on change of shareholding of start-ups from seven years of incorporation to ten years.
- Deduction from capital gains on investment in residential house under sections 54 and 54 F to be capped at Rs. 10 crore for better targeting of tax concessions and exemptions.
- Proposal to limit income tax exemption from proceeds of insurance policies with very high value. Where aggregate of premium for life insurance policies (other than ULIP) issued on or after 1st April, 2023 is above Rs. 5 lakh, income from only those policies with aggregate premium up to Rs. 5 lakh shall be exempt.
- Income of authorities, boards and commissions set up by statutes of the Union or State for the purpose of housing, development of cities, towns and villages, and regulating, or regulating and developing an activity or matter, proposed to be exempted from income tax.
- Minimum threshold of Rs. 10,000/- for TDS to be removed and taxability relating to online gaming to be clarified. Proposal to provide for TDS and taxability on net winnings at the time of withdrawal or at the end of the financial year.
- Conversion of gold into electronic gold receipt and vice versa not to be treated as capital gain.
- TDS rate to be reduced from 30 per cent to 20 per cent on taxable portion of EPF withdrawal in non-PAN cases.
- Income from Market Linked Debentures to be taxed.
- Deployment of about 100 Joint Commissioners for disposal of small appeals in order to reduce the pendency of appeals at Commissioner level.
- Increased selectivity in taking up appeal cases for scrutiny of returns already received this year.

- Period of tax benefits to funds relocating to IFSC, GIFT City extended till 31.03.2025.
- Certain acts of omission of liquidators under section 276 A of the Income Tax Act to be decriminalized with effect from 1st April, 2023.
- Carry forward of losses on strategic disinvestment including that of IDBI Bank to be allowed.
- Agniveer Fund to be provided EEE status. The payment received from the Agniveer Corpus Fund by the Agniveers enrolled in Agnipath Scheme, 2022 proposed to be exempt from taxes. Deduction in the computation of total income is proposed to be allowed to the Agniveer on the contribution made by him or the Central Government to his Seva Nidhi account.

Indirect Taxes

- Number of basic customs duty rates on goods, other than textiles and agriculture, reduced to 13 from 21.
- Minor changes in the basic custom duties, cesses and surcharges on some items including toys, bicycles, automobiles and naphtha.
- Excise duty exempted on GST-paid compressed bio gas contained in blended compressed natural gas.
- Customs Duty on specified capital goods/machinery for manufacture of lithium-ion cell for use in battery of electrically operated vehicle (EVs) extended to 31.03 .2024
- Customs duty exempted on vehicles, specified automobile parts/components, sub-systems and tyres when imported by notified testing agencies, for the purpose of testing and/ or certification, subject to conditions.
- Customs duty on camera lens and its inputs/parts for use in manufacture of camera module of cellular mobile phone reduced to zero and concessional duty on lithium-ion cells for batteries extended for another year. - Basic customs duty reduced on parts of open cells of TV panels to 2.5 per cent.

- Basic customs duty on electric kitchen chimney increased to 15 per cent from 7.5 per cent.
- Basic customs duty on heat coil for manufacture of electric kitchen chimneys reduced to 15 per cent from 20 per cent.
- Denatured ethyl alcohol used in chemical industry exempted from basic customs duty.
- Basic customs duty reduced on acid grade fluorspar (containing by weight more than 97 per cent of calcium fluoride) to 2.5 per cent from 5 per cent.
- Basic customs duty on crude glycerin for use in manufacture of epicholorhydrin reduced to 2.5 per cent from 7.5 per cent.
- Duty reduced on key inputs for domestic manufacture of shrimp feed.
- Basic customs duty reduced on seeds used in the manufacture of lab grown diamonds.
- Duties on articles made from dore and bars of gold and platinum increased.
- Import duty on silver dore, bars and articles increased.
- Basic Customs Duty exemption on raw materials for manufacture of CRGO Steel, ferrous scrap and nickel cathode continued.
- Concessional BCD of 2.5 per cent on copper scrap is continued.
- Basic customs duty rate on compounded rubber increased to 25 per cent from 10 per cent or 30 per kg whichever is lower.
- National Calamity Contingent Duty (NCCD) on specified cigarettes revised upwards by about 16 per cent.

Legislative Changes in Customs Laws

- Customs Act, 1962 to be amended to specify a time limit of nine months from date of filing application for passing final order by Settlement Commission.

- Customs Tariff Act to be amended to clarify the intent and scope of provisions relating to Anti-Dumping Duty (ADD), Countervailing Duty (CVD), and Safeguard Measures.

CGST Act to be amended

To raise the minimum threshold of tax amount for launching prosecution under GST from one crore to two crore to reduce the compounding amount from the present range of 50 to 150 per cent of tax amount to the range of 25 to 100 per cent decriminalise certain offences, to restrict filing of returns/statements to a maximum period of three years from the due date of filing of the relevant return/statement; and to enable unregistered suppliers and composition taxpayers to make intra-state supply of goods through ECommerce Operators (ECOs). Fund Allocation for Ministry:

- Ministry of Defence-594 lacs Cr.
- Ministry of Road Transport and Highways-2.70lacs Cr.
- Ministry of Railways-2.41 lacs cr.
- Ministry of Consumer affairs,Food and Public Distribution-2.06 lacs cr.
- Ministry of Home Affairs- 1.96lacs Cr.
- Minsitry of Chemicals and Fertlizers- 1.78 Lacs Cr.
- Ministry of Rural Development- 1.60 lacs Cr.
- Ministry of Agriculture and Farmer's Welfare-1.25 lacs Cr.
- Ministry of Communications-1.23 lacs Cr.

Grammy Awards 2023 Winners List

The Crypto.com Arena in Los Angeles played host to the 65th Annual Grammy Awards ceremony on February 5, 2023. It honoured the top performers, songs, and recordings from the eligibility year, which spanned October 1, 2021, to September 30, 2022. November 15, 2022 saw the announcement of the nominations. The 63rd and 64th ceremonies were presented by South African comedian Trevor Noah, who served as host once more this year.

Let us know all about the 65th Grammy Awards and the Grammy Awards 2023 Winners list:

Key Highlights

- The ceremony honoured three "lost icons": Takeoff, the Migos rapper who was shot and killed in November, one of the glories of country music, who passed away in November, and Christine McVie, the Fleetwood Mac vocalist who passed away in October.

- With nine nominations, Beyoncé is the most nominated artist this year. She announced her 2023 world tour.

- The top nominees also include Carlile (seven nominations), Adele (seven nominations), and Kendrick Lamar (eight nominations each).

- Viola Davis became only the third Black woman in history to acquire the elusive and prestigious EGOT status.

- She won her first Grammy for her reading of her biography "Finding Me" on audiobook.

As the first transgender woman to get a Grammy in the best pop duo/group performance category, Kim Petras created Grammy history. Grammy Awards 2023 Winners List:

A "Golden Book Awards" 2023 Announced

The "Golden Book Awards" is announced its winner for 2023. This prestigious event recognizes and celebrates the best book in literature. There were more than 75,000 books published in India and nominees include a diverse mix of literary genres, including fiction, non-fiction, poetry, and children's books. The awards are judged by a panel of literary experts, like Dr Kailash Pinjani (President Indian Authors Association), Dr Deepak Parbat (Founder of Superfast Author) & Murali Sundaram (Founder of TLC), who choose the winners based on factors such as originality, creativity, and impact on the literary world.

The winners of Golden Book Awards 2023

- J.K Rowling - Fantastic Beasts: The Secrets Of Dumbledore
- Gaur Gopal Das - Energize Your Mind: A Monk's Guide To Mindful Living
- Deepak Chopra - The Seven Spiritual Law Of Success: A Practical Guide To Achieving Your Dreams

- Kamlesh Patel - The Wisdom Bridge: Nine Principles To A Life That Echoes In The Hearts Of Your Loved Ones
- Jeff Kinney - Diary Of A Wimpy Kid: Diper Overlode
- Ashneer Grover - Doglapan: The Hard Truth About Life And Start-Ups
- Ruskin Bond - How To Live Your Life
- Namita Thapar - The Dolphin And The Shark: Stories On Entrepreneurship
- Sneh Desai, Sunil Tulsiani & Brian Tracy - Ultimate Secrets To Wealth
- Raj Shamani - Build, Don't Talk - Things You Wish You Were Taught In School
- Bhupendra Singh Raathore - The Magic Of Thinking Rich
- Deepak Bajaj - Network Marketing In 60 Minutes
- Deepti Naval - A Country Called Childhood: A Memoir
- Smita Goswamy - Family Run To Family Led
- Subadra Ilan - An Enticing Career
- Aadya Dube - Always Be Unique
- Navin Reuben Dawson - Chimaera
- Rajeev Kumar Dubey - Urvi
- Dr Soumendra Nath Bandyopadhyay - The Mysteries of The Universe-Where Fact Is More Interesting Than Fiction
- Ankush Pare - Secret to overcome stammering and becoming an effective speaker
- Parag Pandya - Padagha (Japanese Version Bussokusekika)
- Moasenla R. Jamir - Foreign Engine In Flight - A Light Of Passage In Poems
- Gowri Venket - Superstar Of My Life - Saibaba
- Dr Sreeveni V - Self-Worth As Your First Impression Signature Of Your Expression
- Ashutosh Madhukar Marathe - The Extra In Ordinary
- Dr K. Sreekumar - Buddhavelicham
- Rakhi Kapoor - Now You Breathe - Overcoming Toxic Relationships And Abuse
- Chandrima Chowdhury - The Tales Of The Uncommon Commons
- Dr P. Madhurima Reddy - The Awakening
- Aashish Patidar Property Shastra - A Vedic Guide To Buy The Right Property
- S. Ilanchezhiyan - 10x Ceo To The Board Joy To Yoy
- Kiran Sidde - Vidyarthi-Betal
- Osama Regaah - Travel And Thoughts

About the Golden Book Awards

Golden Book Awards is sponsored by Wings Publication International; they have a presence in many countries, and they are supporting literature and upcoming authors in the entire world. Wings Publication supports entrepreneurs, coaches, trainers & consultants to establish authority and thought leadership in form of the book. They are constantly seeking new ways to build your brand and showcase your expertise. One often overlooked opportunity for doing so is by writing a book.

Now there remain only two vacancies at the Supreme Court, which could be filled in the coming days if SC Collegium's January 31 proposal to elevate Allahabad High Court Chief Justice Rajesh Bindal and Gujarat High Court Chief Justice Aravind Kumar as SC judges, is accepted by the president.

The 5 newly appointed judges are:

- Justice Pankaj Mithal, the chief justice of Rajasthan High Court
- Justice Sanjay Karol, the chief justice of Patna High Court
- Justice PV Sanjay Kumar, the chief justice of Manipur High Court
- Justice Ahsanuddin Amanullah, a judge of Patna High Court
- Justice Manoj Misra, a judge of Allahabad High Court

Timeline of These Appointment:

- The Supreme Court collegium had recommended the names of these judge for elevation on December 13.

- The notification came a day after the Supreme Court had pulled up the Union government for delaying the appointments. The court had given the Centre 10 days to process the appointments, after, after Attorney General N Venkataramani had said that it would be done soon.

- In the past few months, the Collegium has been releasing more information in public about its rationale for recommending judges, names pending with the government and inputs of intelligence agencies on judicial appointments.

- On January 24, Union law minister Kiren Rijiju said that the releasing of certain portions of sensitive reports of the Intelligence Bureau and the Research and Analysis Wing was a "matter of grave concern".

- Traditionally, discussions that took place during collegium meetings were not recorded or released in any form, and only the names of the recommended candidates were released in the public domain.

RBI Monetary Policy February 2023

Reserve Bank of India (RBI) Governor Shaktikanta Das released the Monetary Policy statement, which included the highly anticipated increase in the repo rate of 25 basis points. The central bank had increased the important benchmark interest rate by 35 basis points in its December monetary policy review (bps). In order to keep inflation under control, the Reserve Bank has raised the short-term lending rate by 250 basis points, including the rate in effect today.

Following are the revised rates in the RBI Monetary Policy 2023:

- Repo Rate: 6.50%
- Standing Deposit Facility (SDF): 6.25%
- Marginal Standing Facility (MSF): 6.75%

Important Takeaways from RBI Monetary Policy Q1 FY23:

- Governor Shaktikanta Das Core inflation has not changed. As of January 27, 2023, non-food credit growth was up 16.7% from the prior corresponding period. In order to reduce the CPI, we must never waver.

- As the policy likely defied expectations of a dovish turn, bonds declined, with the yield on benchmark 10-year notes jumping by as far as four basis points to 7.36%, while the currency was trading higher.

- In 12 cities, RBI will roll out a prototype programme for coin-operated machines that use QR codes.

- After the RBI policy announcement, the Sensex was trading almost 300 points higher and the Nifty was up 0.6%.

- Current account deficit will remain eminently controllable and moderate in the second half of 20222023: RBI Governor

- In 2022 and thus far this year, the Indian Rupee has remained the least volatile of its Asian counterparts: RBI Governor

- According to the RBI Governor, a rate increase of 25bps is acceptable at this time, and monetary policy should remain flexible and responsive to inflation.

- According to the RBI, retail inflation will be 6.5% instead of 6.7% in FY23 and 5.3% in FY24.

- Estimated growth of the gross domestic product (GDP) for FY23 was raised to 7% from 6.8%. - The RBI anticipates 6.4% GDP growth for 2023-2024.

- Rate adjustment for the SDF (Standing Deposit Facility) to 6.25% from 6%.

- Early trading sees the Indian rupee gain 4 paise to 82.66 against the US dollar as traders assess Jerome Powell's remarks and wait for the Reserve Bank of India to announce its policy.

Here are the inflation rate projections by the RBI Monetary Policy:

- FY23 Inflation Rate Projection: 6.5%
- Inflation FY23: 6.5%
- Inflation Average (Jan-March FY23): 5.6%
- Inflation FY24 Projection: 5.3%
- Real GDP Growth FY24: 6.4%

World Happiness Index 2023

The World Happiness Index 2023 Report will mark its tenth anniversary with this year's Globe Happiness Reflect, which uses data from international surveys to show how people rank their lives in more than 150 countries. In these dark times, there is a glimmer of optimism revealed by the World Happiness Index 2023. The pandemic not only caused anguish and suffering, but it also led to a rise in social assistance and charitable giving.

Rank	Country	Happiness Index 2023	Population in 2022

1.	Finland	7.842	5,554,960
2.	Denmark	7.62	5,834,950
3.	Switzerland	7.571	8,773,637
4.	Iceland	7.554	345,393
5.	Netherlands	7.464	17,211,447
6.	Norway	7.392	5,511,370
7.	Sweden	7.363	10,218,971
8.	Luxembourg	7.324	642,371
9.	New Zealand	7.277	4,898,203
10.	Austria	7.268	9,066,710
136.	India	**3.819**	**1,406,631,776**

Finland was named the world's happiest country for the fifth year in a row, according to the World Happiness Report.

- The Sustainable Development Solutions Network of the UN has published a new report, which was made public two days prior to the yearly International Day of Happiness.
- It rates 150 countries (146 in 2023) based on factors such as GDP, life expectancy, and other indicators of quality of life.
- The ranking, now in its eleventh year, assigns a score between 0 and 10 based on an average of data gathered over three years and a mathematical formula.
- According to a yearly UN survey released, Russia is not having a happy year as it drops in the global happiness rankings again this year.
- According to factors that contribute to happiness, such as GDP per capita, social support, healthy life expectancy, social freedom, charity, and lack of corruption, the World Happiness Report ranks 156 nations.

President Draupadi Murmu named new governors in 12 states and 1UT

President of India Droupadi Murmu appointed 13 new Governors while accepting the resignations of Bhagat Singh Koshyari as Governor of Maharashtra and of Radha Krishnan Mathur as Lt. Governor of Ladakh on 12 February. Following is the complete list of new governors who have been appointed. These appointments will take effect from the dates they assume charge of their respective offices :-

The fresh appointments

State	Name
Governor of Arunachal Pradesh	Lt. General Kaiwalya Trivikram Patnaik (Retired)
Governor of Sikkim	Lakshman Prasad Acharya
Governor of Jharkhand	C P Radhakrishnan
Governor of Himachal Pradesh	Shiv Pratap Shukla
Governor of Assam	Gulab Chand Kataria
Governor of Andhra Pradesh	S. Abdul Nazeer

Change of states of some current governors

State	Name
Governor of Andhra Pradesh appointed as Governor of Chhattisgarh	Justice (Retd) Biswa Bhusan Harichandan
Governor of Chhattisgarh appointed as Governor of Manipur	Anusuiya Uikye
Governor of Manipur appointed as Governor of Nagaland	La. Ganesan
Governor of Bihar appointed as Governor of Meghalaya	Phagu Chauhan
Governor of Himachal Pradesh appointed as Governor of Bihar Arlekar	Rajendra Vishwanath

Governor of Arunachal Pradesh appointed as Lt. Governor of Ladakh (Retd)	Brig (Dr) B D Mishra
Governor of Jharkhand appointed as Governor of Maharashtra	Ramesh Bais

Shuman Gill and Grace Scrivens named ICC Men's and Women's Player of January

India batter Shuman Gill was named ICC Men's Player of the Month for January following a series of impressive innings in the ODI format, while England U-19 skipper Grace Scrivens became the youngest player to be named for the women's honour. The awards were decided in a global vote conducted among media representatives, ICC Hall of Famers, former international players, and fans registered at the ICC website.

ICC Men's Player of the Month, January 2023 - Shuman Gill

India's Shuman Gill wins his first ICC Men's Player of the Month award following another fine series of performances in ODI cricket. With 567 runs during January, which included three century-plus scores, the 23-year-old batter wowed fans with a lethal combination of graceful and attacking stroke play.

Gill overcomes a competitive field to claim the award, beating New Zealand opener Devon Conway and compatriot Mohammed Siraj in the global vote. In doing so, he becomes the first Indian winner since Virat Kohli in October 2022.

ICC Women's Player of the Month, January 2023 - Grace Scrivens

Scrivens bagged the award after her all-round brilliance in the inaugural ICC U-19 Women's T20 World Cup. Equally, the England captain excelled in her leadership role, guiding her side to the final, only to lose to eventual title winners India. Captaining her side in seven outings, the 19-year-old enjoyed plenty of success in the middle, scoring 293 runs at an average of 41.85 which included three successive halfcenturies in victories over Rwanda, Ireland and the West Indies.

ICC Men's Player of the Previous Month

- January 2022: Keegan Petersen (South Africa)
- February 2022: Shreyas Iyer (India)
- March 2022: Babar Azam (Pakistan)
- April 2022: Keshav Maharaj (South Africa)
- May 2022: Angelo Mathews (Sri Lanka)
- June 2022: Jonny Bairstow (England)
- July 2022: Prabath Jayasuriya (Sri Lanka)
- August 2022: Sikandar Raza (Zimbabwe)
- September 2022: Mohammad Rizwan (Pakistan)
- October 2022: Virat Kohli (India)
- November 2022: Jos Buttler (England)
- December 2022: Harry Brook (England)

ICC Women's Player of the Previous Month

- January 2022: Heather Knight (England)
- February 2022: Amelia Kerr (New Zealand)
- March 2022: Rachael Haynes (Australia)
- April 2022: Alyssa Healy (Australia)
- May 2022: Tuba Hassan (Pakistan)
- June 2022: Marizanne Kapp (South Africa)
- July 2022: Emma Lamb (England)
- August 2022: Tahlia McGrath (Australia)
- September 2022: Harmanpreet Kaur (India)
- October 2022: Nida Dar (Pakistan)
- November 2022: Sidra Ameen (Pakistan)
- December 2022: Ashleigh Gardner (Australia)

5th Khelo India Youth Games 2022

The fifth edition of the Khelo India Youth Games conclude on February 11. In the Khelo India Youth Games - 2022, Maharashtra was the overall champion by securing a total of 161 medals including 56 gold, 55 silver and 50 bronze medals. On the other hand, Haryana has been at the second position by getting a total of 128 medals including 41 gold, 32 silver and 55 bronze. Host Madhya Pradesh finished third with 96 medals including 39 gold.

- The Games were hosted in Madhya Pradesh from 31 January 2023 to 11 February 2023. For the first time water sports namely Kayaking Canoeing, Canoe Salam and Fencing were part of this edition of Khelo India Games. It was organized in eight different cities of the state.
- These eight host cities are Bhopal, Indore, Jabalpur, Gwalior, Ujjain, Maheshwar, Mandla and Balaghat.
- Over 5,000 athletes from 36 states and union territories of India participated in the Khelo India Youth Games 2022. Where athletes competed for 973 medals - 295 gold, 295 silver and 383 bronze - in 27 sports. The participation of girls in these games was about 40 percent.

Khelo India Youth Games: Medal Tally

Rank	State	Gold	Silver	Bronze	Total
1	Maharashtra	56	55	50	161
2	Haryana	41	32	55	128
3	Madhya Pradesh	39	30	27	96
4	Rajasthan	19	10	19	48
5	Delhi	16	22	26	64
6	Kerala	15	12	19	46
7	Manipur	13	9	12	34
8	Tamil Nadu	12	19	21	52
9	Odisha	11	8	11	30
10	Punjab	11	7	15	33

76th BAFTA Awards 2023

At the Royal Festival Hall in London, England, the 76th British Academy Film Awards, also referred to as the BAFTAs, were presented. The award was hosted by actor Richard E Grant, the star-studded ceremony saw the German ant-war film All Quiet on the Western Front winning seven awards, including the two big wins awards, Best Film and Best Director. Shaunak Sen's documentary All That Breathes from India was a nominee for the Best Documentary award, which went to Daniel Roher's

Here are the complete list of winners:

Category	**Winner**
Best Film	All Quiet on the Western Front
Leading Actress	Cate Blanchett, Tar
Leading Actor	Austin Butler, Elvis
Best Director	Edward Berger, All Quiet on the Western Front
Best Casting	Elvis
Best Cinematography	All Quiet on the Western Front
Adapted Screenplay	All Quiet on The Western Front, Edward Berger, Lesley Paterson, Ian Stokell
Editing	Everything Everywhere All At Once, Paul Rogers
Cinematography	All Quiet On The Western Front, James Friend
Best Documentary	Navalny (Daniel Roher)
EE Bafta Rising Star Award	Emma Mackey
Film Not In The English Language	All Quiet On The Western Front
Best Costume Design	Catherine Martin, Elvis
British Short Film	An Irish Goodbye
Make up & Hair	Elvis; Jason Baird, Mark Coulier, Louise Coulston, Shane Thomas

Production design	Babylon; Florencia Martin, Anthony Carlino
Sound	All Quiet On The Western Front; Lars Ginzsel, Frank Kruse, Viktor Prášil, Markus Stemler
Original Score	All Quiet On The Western Front; Volker Bertelmann
Supporting Actress	Kerry Condon, The Banshees of Inisherin
Supporting Actor	Barry Keoghan, The Banshees of Inisherin

About BAFTA

BAFTA - the British Academy of Film and Television Arts - is a world-leading independent arts charity that brings the very best work in film, games and television to public attention and supports the growth of creative talent in the UK and internationally. Through its Awards ceremonies and yearround programme of learning events and initiatives - which includes workshops, masterclasses, scholarships, lectures and mentoring schemes in the UK, USA and Asia - BAFTA identifies and celebrates excellence, discovers, inspires and nurtures new talent, and enables learning and creative collaboration.

Dadasaheb Phalke International Film Festival Awards 2023

The Dadasaheb Phalke Award is the country's highest award in the field of cinema. The 2023 winners were revealed by the Directorate of Film Festivals. Mumbai will host the 2023 Dadasaheb Phalke International Film Festival ceremony. Alia Bhatt and Ranbir Kapoor won the Best Actor and Best Actress awards at the Dadasaheb Phalke International Film Festival Awards.

Here is the complete list of winners

Category	Winner
Best Film	The Kashmir Files
Film Of The Year	RRR

Best Actor	Ranbir Kapoor (Brahmastra Part One: Shiva)
Best Actress	Alia Bhatt (Gangubhai Khatiawadi)
Critics Best Actor	Varun Dhawan (Bhediya)
Critics Best Actress	Vidya Balan (Jalsa)
Best Director	R Balki (Chup)
Best Cinematographer	PS Vinod (Vikram Vedha)
Most Promising Actor	Rishab Shetty (Kantara)
Best Actor In A Supporting Role	Manish Paul (Jugjugg Jeeyo)
Best Playback Singer (Male)	Sachet Tandon (Maiyya Mainu - Jersey)
Best Playback Singer (Female)	Neeti Mohan (Meri Jaan - Gangubhai Khatiawadi)
Best Web Series	Rudra: The Edge Of Darkness (Hindi)
Most Versatile Actor	Anupam Kher (The Kashmir Files)
Television Series Of The Year	Anupamaa
Best Actor In A Television Series	Zain Imam for Fanaa (Ishq Mein Marjawaan)

Best Actress In A Television Series	Tejasswi Prakash (Naagin)
Dadasaheb Phalke International Film Festival Awards 2023 for Outstanding Contribution In The Film Industry	Rekha
Dadasaheb Phalke International Film Festival Awards 2023 for Outstanding Contribution In The Music Industry	Hariharan

About the Dadasaheb Phalke Award

The Dadasaheb Phalke Award is India's highest award in the field of cinema. It is presented annually at the National Film Awards ceremony by the Directorate of Film Festivals, an organisation set up by the Ministry of Information and Broadcasting. The recipient is honoured for their "outstanding contribution to the growth and development of Indian cinema" and is selected by a committee consisting of eminent personalities from the Indian film industry. The award comprises a Swarna Kamal (Golden Lotus) medallion, a shawl, and a cash prize of ₹1,000,000 (US $13,000).

Sansad Ratna award 2023

13 members of Parliament (MP) have been nominated for the Sansad Ratna Awards 2023. The Jury Committee of eminent Parliamentarians and civil society, chaired by Arjun Ram Meghwal (State Minister of Parliamentary Affairs) and Co-Chaired by T S Krishnamurthy (Former Chief Election Commissioner of India) has nominated eight MPs from Lok Sabha and five from Rajya Sabha for the Sansad Ratna Awards 2023. These nominations are based on cumulative performance in questions, private members' bills and members' debates from the beginning of the 17th Lok Sabha till the end of the Winter Session 2022.
Notably: The 13th Sansad Ratna Awards 2023 will be presented on March 25 in the national Capital.

Sansad Ratna Awards 2023 nominated from Lok Sabha

1 Adhir Ranjan Chowdhury (INC, West Bengal),
2 Gopal Chinayya Shetty (BJP, Maharashtra),

3 Sudhir Gupta (BJP, Madhya Pradesh) and
4 Dr. Amol Ramsing Kolhe (NCP, Maharashtra)
5 Bidyut Baran Mahato (BJP, Jharkhand),
6 Dr. Sukanta Majumdar (BJP, West Bengal),
7 Kuldeep Rai Sharma (INC, Andaman Nicobar Islands),
8 Dr Heena Vijayakumar Gavit (BJP, Maharashtra),

Sansad Ratna Awards 2023 from Rajya Sabha

1 Smt Fauzia Tahseen Ahmed Khan (NCP, Maharashtra)
2 Dr. John Brittas (CPI-M, Kerala),
3 Dr. Manoj Kumar Jha (RJD, Bihar),
4 Vishambhar Prasad Nishad (Samajwadi Party, UP) and
5 Smt Chhaya Verma (INC, Chhattisgarh)

Two Parliamentary Committees of Lok Sabha nominated for Sansad Ratna Award 2023

1 Rajya Sabha's Standing Committee on Tourism, Transport, and Culture, chaired by Vijay Sai Reddy
2 Lok Sabha's Parliamentary Committee on Finance, chaired by Jayant Sinha

Lifetime Achievement Award

- Dr APJ Abdul Kalam Lifetime Achievement Award: T K Rangarajan, (Former Rajya Sabha MP for two terms and a Senior CPIM Leader).

Some facts about Sansad Ratna Awards:

Sansad Ratna Awards were instituted on the suggestion of Dr APJ Abdul Kalam to honour top performing Parliamentarians. He himself inaugurated the first edition of the award ceremony in 2010 in Chennai. So far, 90 top performing parliamentarians have been honoured and all of them have received the award individually. K. Srinivasan is the Founder Chairman of the Sansad Ratna Award Committee and Ms. Priyadarshini Rahul is the Chairman.

ICC Women's T20 World Cup 2023

ICC Women's T20 World Cup Final: Australia won the Women's T20 World Cup for the sixth time when they beat South Africa by 19 runs in the final at Newlands. Opening batter Beth Mooney anchored the Australian innings, scoring an unbeaten 74 in a total of 156 for six. Victory for the Aussies is their sixth in Women's T20 World Cup history and completes a hat-trick of tournament wins under captain Meg Lanning after their triumphs in 2018 and 2020. Australia's previous victories came in 2010, 2012, 2014, 2018 and 2020.

ICC Women's T20 World Cup

Australia's Ashleigh Gardner is the winner of the ICC Player of the Tournament award. The outstanding Gardner took ten wickets and smashed 110 runs in Australia's triumphant campaign, playing a huge part in helping the team to a sixth Women's T20 World Cup title.

- Beth Mooney is Player of the Match for her excellent half-century. Beth Mooney top-scored with 74*.

ICC Women's T20 World Cup: Brief scores

- Australia 156-6 in 20 overs (B. Mooney 74 not out; S. Ismail 2-26, M. Kapp 2-35) vs South Africa 137-6 in 20 overs (L. Wolvaardt 61).
- Result: Australia won by 19 runs
- Toss: Australia

Banking and Financial Current Affairs

- Digital payments across the country registered a growth of 24.13 per cent in a year through September 2022, as per the RBI's Digital Payments Index which measures the adoption of online transactions. The newly-constituted RBI's Digital Payments Index (RBIDPI) stood at 377.46 in September 2022 against 349.30 in March 2022 and 304.06 in September 2021. The index is published on a semi-annual basis(i.e. twice a year) from March 2021 onwards with a lag of four months.

- According to the RBI's most recent status report, there were approximately 1.87 crore physical and digital payment acceptance devices deployed under the Payments Infrastructure Development Fund (PIDF) Scheme as of December 31, 2022.

- HDFC Bank, one of the leading private sector banks of India, has partnered with National Institute of Information Technology (NIIT) Limited, a global talent development corporation, to build a large pool of skilled Virtual Relationship Management professionals for the banking industry. Virtual Relationship managers (VRMs) act as one point of contact for all requirements or issues of bank's managed customers.

- Airtel Payments Bank announced the availability of its current account, BizKhata, which offers small businesses and business partners across the nation fast activation and limitless transactions. Because they cannot maintain the minimum amount required for business accounts, many small business owners continue to use savings accounts for business-related expenses. This makes it difficult to distinguish between personal and corporate dealings.

- Edelweiss General Insurance has rebranded itself as Zuno General Insurance Limited (Zuno GI), which is a new age digital insurer with an aspiration to reimagine and redefine Insurance to make it easy, friendly, and transparent.

- The Reserve Bank of India decided to expand the scope of the Trade Receivable Discounting System or the TReDS platform allowing the use of insurance facilities, permitting entities eligible to undertake factoring business to participate as financiers on TReDS and allowing secondary market operations on the platform. The central bank's decision is expected to boost trade of receivables increasing cash flows to MSMEs.

- Shaktikanta Das, the governor of the RBI, announced that a pilot programme to introduce coin vending machines that use QR codes will begin shortly. In response to the outcome of the monetary policy for the year 2023, the Central Bank Governor announced that the RBI will introduce a coin vending machine that uses a QR code to improve accessibility to coins.

- According to Telecom and IT Minister Ashwini Vaishnaw, the government has said that it will provide a digital credit facility this year in a similar manner to how it introduced the Unified Payments Interface (UPI). Even modest street sellers will be able to use the programme to obtain credit from banks.

- Indore Municipal Corporation (IMC) has launched India's first public issue of municipal bonds intending to raise up to Rs 244 crore to fund a solar power project.

This would be the first time a municipal body is targeting individual investors in India.

- The "Digital Payments Utsav," a comprehensive campaign aiming at encouraging digital payments throughout India, was launched by Shri Ashwini Vaishnaw, Minister for Electronics and Information Technology, Communications, and Railways.

- The third dedicated branch for start-ups in the nation has been established by State Bank of India (SBI) in Gurugram. Dinesh Kumar Khara, the chairman of SBI, declared during the branch's inauguration on Thursday that it will offer start-ups comprehensive support from entity formation through the issuance of IPOs and FPOs. Gurugram is home to the third-highest number of unicorns-startups valued at $100 billion or more-in India, behind Bengaluru and Mumbai. RBI's 'Financial Literacy Week' started on 13th and will last till February 17, 2023. The Reserve Bank of India (RBI) has been conducting this every year since 2016 to propagate financial education messages on a particular theme among members of public across the country. Last year, RBI observed 'financial literacy week' from February 14 to February 18, 2022. The central bank held an event to propagate financial education messages on the theme of "Go Digital Go Secure".

- The government has said that it proposes to set up a Bima Sugam portal to address the existing protection gap across life, health and general insurance businesses in the country. Replying to a question in the Lok Sabha, Finance Minister Nirmala Sitharaman said that the Insurance Regulatory and Development Authority of India (IRDAI) has informed that the portal will be an insurance market infrastructure, where insurers, distribution networks and the policy holders would virtually meet across a seamless digital platform.

- The Reserve Bank announced its second global hackathon - 'HARBINGER 2023 - Innovation for Transformation' with the theme 'Inclusive Digital Services'. Registration for the hackathon starts from February 22, 2023. It had received 363 proposals submitted by teams from within India and from 22 other countries including the US, UK, Sweden, Singapore, Philippines, and Israel.

- The Reserve Bank of India said it has cancelled the registration of Pune-based Kudos Finance and Investments and Mumbai-based Credit Gate for regulatory lapses in lending practices. With cancelled Certificate of Registration(CoR), the two NBFCs should not transact the business of a non-banking financial institution, the RBI said in a statement.

- Paytm Payments Banks Limited (PPBL) has launched Unified Payments Interface (UPI) LITE, enabled by National Payments Corporation of India (NPCI) for multiple small-value UPI transactions. This feature will help with faster real-time transactions with a single click through Paytm as the bank aims to drive the adoption of digital payments across the country. As a part of its efforts to drive innovation, the Bank said it is the first payments bank to launch such UPI LITE feature.

- The RBI has granted a total of 32 in-principle authorisations to existing payment aggregators, to operate as online payment aggregators, according to a press statement issued by the central bank. RBI also granted a total of 19 new online PA authorisations to firms including Groww Pay Services, Juspay Technologies, Mswipe Technologies, Tata Payments, and Zoho Payment Tech. - Karnataka Bank was awarded with 'Prathista Puraskar' under 'Digidhan Awards 2021-22' by Ministry of Electronics and Information Technology (MeitY), government of India for achieving target with highest percentage in BHIM-UPI transactions in private sector bank category.

- ICICI Bank and BNP Paribas have signed an initial pact to cater to the banking requirements of European corporates operating in India and Indian companies in the European Union. The Memorandum of Understanding (MoU) between the two entities establishes a framework of a partnership between the two banks for providing financial services to corporate customers operating in the India, Europe corridor, private sector lender ICICI Bank.

- The Reserve Bank of India (RBI) has made changes to the NEFT and RTGS systems for Foreign Contribution (Regulation) Act (FCRA) related transactions following the Home Ministry's order for State Bank of India (SBI) to report details of overseas donors on a daily basis, including the purpose of remittances. Under the FCRA, foreign contributions can only be received in the "FCRA account" of SBI's New Delhi Main Branch, with contributions coming directly from foreign banks through SWIFT and from Indian intermediary banks through NEFT and RTGS systems.

- Public sector Indian Overseas Bank has launched the facility of issuance of e-BG (Electronic Bank Guarantee) scheme in association with the National e-

Governance Services Ltd. The e-BG is an instrument issued by the city-headquartered bank in which the bank undertakes to guarantee a specific amount against the nonfulfillment of some action/performance of the applicant.

- As the US dollar rises due to the speculation that the Federal Reserve will continue to tighten repo rates, it has bogged down the Indian Rupee. The need to tackle a free fall in the value of the Rupee, was bound to trigger a sell off of foreign currency by the Reserve Bank of India. This may have triggered a $8.31 billion in India's foreign exchange reserves for the week that ended on February 10. This has taken the reserves down to $566.94 billion.

- Philips Domestic Appliances has announced the change of its company name to Versuni. The new name 'Versuni' is the next step after the Domestic Appliances business became independent in September 2021. Although the visual identity of the company is changing, its mission to turn houses into homes remains constant.

- Bank of Maharashtra (BoM) has emerged as the top performer among state-owned lenders in terms of loan growth percentage during the third quarter of 2022-23, an analysis of the latest financial results of public sector banks showed. The Pune-based lender recorded a 21.67 per cent increase in gross advances on a year-on-year basis, according to the latest quarterly numbers of the public sector bank (PSB).

- The 190th Meeting of the Employees' State Insurance Corporation (ESIC) was held in Chandigarh under the chairmanship of Shri Bhupender Yadav, Union Minister for Labor & Employment and Environment, Forest, and Climate Change. Shri Rameswar Teli, Minister of State for Labor & Employment, Petroleum & Natural Gas, was present at the meeting as well.

- The Reserve Bank of India (RBI) due to insufficient capital and earning potential revoked the licence of Madhya Pradesh's Garha Co-operative Bank, Guna. According to a statement from the RBI, approximately 98.4% of the depositors of the cooperative bank are eligible to receive the full value of their savings from the Deposit Insurance and Credit Guarantee Corporation (DICGC).

- The Unified Payments Interface (UPI) of India and PayNow of Singapore will be integrated, to facilitate quicker and more affordable cross-border remittance transfers. On February 21, cross-border connectivity would essentially be launched in front of Prime Ministers Lee Hsien Loong of Singapore and Narendra Modi of India.

- The Reserve Bank of India (RBI) appointed Vikramaditya Singh Khichi to a panel to advise the administrator of debt-ridden Reliance Capital (RCap), the apex bank said in a release. Khichi, former executive director of Bank of Baroda, has been appointed to Reliance Capital's advisory committee following the resignation of Srinivasan Varadarajan from the panel.

- Reserve Bank of India vide its Circular dated 16th February, 2023 regarding the introduction of Foreign Contribution (Regulation) Act (FCRA) related transaction code in NEFT and RTGS Systems.

- Brett Schickler had never before considered the possibility of becoming a published novelist. But, after finding out about the ChatGPT artificial intelligence initiative, Schickler believed he had been given a chance.

- The Asian Development Bank (ADB) in order to help India fulfil its most pressing development requirements, pledged up to **$25** billion over the course of the next five years to support social development, climate change, and infrastructure development in India under the PM Gati Shakti project. - Private sector lender Kotak Mahindra Bank went live with 'Kotak fyn', an integrated portal developed to offer comprehensive digital banking and value-added services to its business banking and corporate clients.

- The UK has surpassed India as the sixth-largest equity market in the world for the first time since May 2022 as a weaker pound increases the attraction of exporters and concerns over the Adani-Hindenburg controversy are being felt throughout Indian markets.

- The State Bank of India (SBI) announced a cooperation with PayNow, the city state's online payment system, for cross-border payments, one day after a real-time payments system linkage was formed between India and Singapore utilising the UPI platform.

- HDFC Bank and UAE-based financial services company Lulu Exchange, have partnered to strengthen crossborder payments between India and Gulf Cooperation Council (GCC) region. Both sides have signed a memorandum of understanding

(MoU) to enable remittances to India through HDFC's online and mobile banking powered by LuLu Exchange.

- Saraswat Bank has partnered with Singapore based digital banking solutions provider Tagit to implement omnichannel digital banking solutions for its retail and corporate customers. Under the association, the bank will use Tagit's Mobeix Digital Banking platform to enhance customer experience.

- Karnataka Bank and Paisalo Digital Ltd, a nondeposit-taking NBFC registered with the Reserve Bank of India, have entered into a co-lending arrangement to provide financial support to the small income segment and to give impetus to the micro and small enterprise segment of the country.

- The government has generated assets worth 26,000 crore during FY23, and a pipeline of proposals totaling 1.23 lakh crore is now being processed at various levels. This is in contrast to the aim of **1.6** lakh crore for the current fiscal year.

- Federal Bank has constructed a 100-KWp on-grid solar power plant, at its corporate headquarters in Aluva. Shyam Srinivasan, MD and CEO of the Federal bank, inaugurated the solar facility and called it an important turning point in the organization's sustainable path.

- The National Pension System (NPS), a market-linked, defined contribution plan run by the Pension Fund Regulatory and Development Authority (PFRDA), provides residents with affordable social security. Both companies and employees make contributions to this low-cost, tax-efficient plan. The PFRDA has mandated that users upload certain papers starting on April 1, 2023.

Economy Current Affairs

- The International Monetary Fund (IMF) has informed it is expecting some setbacks in the Indian economy next fiscal year and projected the growth to 6.1 percent from 6.8 percent during the current fiscal ending March 31.

- According to finance ministry Nirmala Sitharaman, the Goods and Services Tax (GST) collection in January 2023 saw a significant increase, reaching over Rs 1.55 lakh crore. This marks the second highest-ever mop-up for the GST collection and demonstrates a growth in the country's economy.

- India's unemployment rate fell to 7.14% in January, the lowest in four months, from 8.30% in the previous month, data from the Centre for Monitoring Indian Economy (CMIE) showed. The urban unemployment rate declined to 8.55% in January from 10.09% in the previous month, while the rural unemployment rate slipped to 6.48% from 7.44%, the data showed.

- India's newly created infrastructure-financing institution is planning a maiden bond issue of 50 billion rupees in the next quarter. The managing director at the National Bank for Financing Infrastructure and Development, India's new development finance institution, Rajkiran Rai informed that the institution aims to test the market in terms of pricing with the small issuance.

- China's Alibaba Group has sold its remaining stake in Indian digital payments firm Paytm for about 13.78 billion rupees ($167.14 million) through a block deal, stock exchange data showed.

- India's foreign exchange reserves saw a drop after nearly three weeks, falling **$1. 5** billion to **$75. 27** billion in the week ended February 3. The fall was the result of the decline in the Foreign Currency Assets (FCA), a major component of the overall reserves, the Reserve Bank of India's weekly statistical supplement said on February 10.

- India's consumer inflation hit a three-month high in January at 6.5%, reversing its downtrend because of higher food prices. The year-on-year increase in the consumer price index (CPI) breached the central bank's upper tolerance limit of 6%, after keeping within targeted range in November and December, according to the Ministry of Statistics and Programme Implementation (MoSPI).

- Gross direct tax collections grew 24 per cent to Rs 15.67 trillion so far this fiscal, the finance ministry said. After adjusting for refunds, the net direct tax collection stood at Rs 12.98 trillion, a growth of 18.40 per cent - India's gross domestic product (GDP) is expected to grow at 6.2 per cent in FY24 as drivers of domestic demand remain intact amid fears of an impending slowdown, Morgan Stanley said in a research report released.

- India's foreign exchange reserves experienced its biggest decline in over 11 months, dropping by 8.3 percent in the week ending February 10, according to the Reserve Bank of India's (RBI) statistical supplement released. After rising for three weeks, forex reserves had started dropping from the week that ended on February 3. This has taken the reserves down to $566.94 billion, of which $500.59 billion are foreign currencies, down $7.11 billion from the previous week.

- The 49th GST Council Meeting was held on 18th February 2023 in New Delhi under the Chairmanship of Finance Minister Nirmala Sitharaman. This meeting is being conducted within a span of three weeks from the Union Budget 2023. The Union Finance Minister, Union Minister of State for Finance Pankaj Chaudhary, besides the finance ministers of states and Union Territories (with legislature) and senior officers from the Union government and states, attended the meeting, according to the finance ministry's official handle.

- IndiaRatings (Ind-Ra) revised its FY24 growth forecast downward to 5.9% from the Reserve Bank of India's 6.4%. The agency predicts that growth would not surpass 6% in 2023-2024 despite factors such as continuing government capital spending, deleverage corporations, reduced NPAs, the Production-Linked Incentive Scheme, and the expectation that global commodity prices will remain stable.

- The NSE has got the greenlight from the capital markets regulator to launch its Social Stock Exchange, the board said. The Securities and Exchange Board of India (Sebi) had given an in-principle approval to National Stock Exchange (NSE) for setting up the exchange last December.

- The second-highest mop-up since the indirect tax levy (GST) was instituted in July 2017 for goods and services tax collection was Rs 1.56 trillion in January 2023. In April 2022, GST receipts reached a record high of Rs 1.68 trillion.

- The country's services exports are doing "extremely well" and going by the current trend these outbound shipments would register about 20 per cent growth in this fiscal and cross the USD **300** billion target despite global economic uncertainties, Commerce and Industry Minister Piyush Goyal has said. - The amount of various subsidies and sops transferred to recipients through direct benefit transfer (DBT) has reached almost Rs **5.5** trillion so far in the current fiscal year, FY23, almost on par with FY21's total and falling just 13% shy of FY22's total achievement.

Business Current Affairs

- Genus Power Infrastructures Ltd. and its 100 percent subsidiary company Hi-Print Metering Solutions Private Limited have received the letter of award (LOA) of Rs 2,855.96 crore for the appointment of Advanced Metering Infrastructure Service Provider (AMISP).

- The Adani Group acquired the strategic Israeli port of Haifa for USD 1.2 billion and vowed to transform the skyline of this Mediterranean city as part of its decision to invest more in the Jewish nation, including opening an artificial intelligence lab in Tel Aviv. Adani Group chairman Gautam Adani, whose business empire was rocked by allegations of fraud by US short seller Hindenburg Research, appeared alongside Israeli Prime Minister Benjamin Netanyahu for signing of the deal to takeover Haifa Port, and spoke of investment opportunities.

- Under fire following allegations of fraud and stock manipulation, the Adani group has received another jolt from the US markets. The group's flagship company Adani Enterprises has been removed from the Dow Jones Sustainability Indices effective February 7. According to a note issued by S&P Dow Jones Indices, home to iconic financial market indicators, the decision to remove Adani Enterprises was taken "following a media & stakeholder analysis".

- Foxconn and Vedanta are close to inducting European chipmaker STMicroelectronics as the technology partner in their proposed semiconductor chip manufacturing unit in India. Foxconn will be the lead partner in the joint venture (JV) that was announced last February. The Vedanta-Foxconn consortium is one of the five applicants seeking government incentives under a $10-billion package announced in December 2021 to promote domestic semiconductor manufacturing.

- Google has invested around $**300** million in Anthropic, an artificial intelligence startup whose technology is said to rival OpenAI, the company behind ChatGPT According to the deal, Anthropic has agreed to purchase some of Google's services to support its technology. The terms of the deal, through which Google will take a stake of about 10 per cent, requires Anthropic to use the money to buy computing resources from the search company's cloud computing division.

- In Mumbai, an industry first for banks and NBFCs, Mobicule, a specialist in debt collection, has announced the release of its mCollect Repossession module. As a component of its debt collection and recovery product, the ground-breaking Asset Repossession Solution is a comprehension solution that maps all the intricate steps involved in the repossession of an asset.

- In the process of the adoption of the Central Bank of Digital Currency (CDDC), Reliance Retail started accepting digital rupees or e-rupee for payments at its store. The payment through digital currency has been started in Reliance Retail's Freshpik store in Mumbai but will soon be expanded to other 17,000 stores of India's largest retailer.
- The government has approved conversion of over Rs 16,133 crore interest dues of debt-ridden Vodafone Idea into equity, after receiving a firm commitment from Aditya Birla Group to run the company and bring necessary investment, telecom minister Ashwini Vaishnaw said. Equity shares of face value of Rs 10 each will be issued to the government at the same price.

- Reliance Industries Limited (RIL) and Ashok Leyland unveiled India's first Hydrogen Internal Combustion Engine (H2-ICE) technology solution for heavy duty trucks. This technology was flagged off by PM Modi at the India Energy Week in Bengaluru. The Hydrogen tech solution will emit near zero emissions, deliver performance on par with conventional diesel trucks and reduce noise and with projected reductions in operating costs thus redefining the future of green mobility.

- PhonePe announced the debut of a service that will enable its Indian users who are travelling overseas to pay foreign businesses using the Unified Payments Interface (UPI). "UPI international" enables retail locations with a native QR (quick response) code in the UAE, Singapore, Mauritius, Nepal, and Bhutan. Similar to how they do with overseas debit cards, users would be able to make direct payments in a foreign currency from their Indian bank. The Walmart-backed finance app PhonePe claimed to be the first to do so in India.

- India's leading fintech, MobiKwik has become the first fintech apps to support RuPay Credit Cards on UPI. The development brings a new level of convenience to the millions of Indians who use UPI for their daily transactions. With nearly 50 million users possessing one or more credit cards, this is a significant milestone in India's drive towards a cashless economy. - During 2021-22, India received foreign inward remittances of USD 89,127 million which was the highest ever inward remittances received in a single year. This was stated by Union Minister of State for Finance Pankaj Chaudhary in a written reply to a question in Rajya Sabha.

- Tata Group is set to record the highest growth in its history, with both unlisted and listed entities growing upwards of 20%. Importantly, both traditional and new businesses have lined up large capex plans. Traditional businesses will fund their own growth through internal accruals.

- In honour of India's G20 presidency and the nation's prominence in mobile payments, One97 Communications Limited, the owner of the top payments and financial services startup Paytm, unveiled a special G20-themed QR Code.

- United States President Joe Biden hailed Air India's decision to purchase over 220 aircraft from Boeing and called it a "historic agreement between Tata-owned airlines and Boeing. This purchase will support over one million American jobs across 44 states, and many will not require a four-year college degree. This announcement also reflects the strength of US-India economic partnership," Joe Biden said in an official statement.
- The public sector oil refineries in India are estimated to build green hydrogen capacity of 137,000 (1.37 lakh) tonnes per annum (TPA) by 2030. If fructified, besides boosting the economy with investments and jobs, this massive capacity building in the green hydrogen sector would reduce greenhouse gas emissions in a large way.

- Rolls-Royce, a British engineering company, announced that it has received an order from Air India for 68 Trent XWB-97 engines, in addition to an option for 20 more. The large A350 aircraft of Airbus are powered by Rolls-Royce XWB engines. Air India sealed an order for procuring 250 Airbus passenger jets. The order comprises 40 Airbus A350s and 210 Airbus A320/321 aircraft. Separately, Air India ordered 220 planes from Boeing.

- According to the Board of Control for Cricket in India, the Tata Group has secured the title sponsorship rights for the Women's Premier League (WPL) for five seasons (BCCI). From February 15, 2023, to July 31, 2027, or up until 30 days after the conclusion of the WPL Season 2027, the salt to software conglomerate will hold the title sponsorship rights.

- E-commerce giant Amazon announced that it will join the Indian government's ONDC (Open Network for Digital Commerce) platform, and as part of its initial collaboration will integrate its Smart Commerce and logistics services with the ONDC network.

- Nokia will no longer use the colour blue and will instead use whatever is more fitting given the circumstances, therefore no particular colour scheme is allocated. Nokia is now a "enterprise technology company," according to Lundmark, rather than just a maker of smartphones.

- Tata group-owned Air India's order for a record **470** aircraft from Airbus and Boeing Co will be at a list price of $70 billion, Chief Executive Campbell Wilson said, as the airline seeks opportunities to expand in longhaul international.

International Current Affairs

- India and the United States launched a programme to enhance their strategic partnership with delegations led by the National Security Advisor (NSA) Ajit Doval and his American counterpart, Jake Sullivan at their meeting in Washington for the inaugural dialogue of the Initiative on Critical and Emerging Technologies (iCET).

- Inflation has risen to a 48-year high in crisis-hit Pakistan, where the International Monetary Fund (IMF) is visiting for urgent talks, according to data released on February 1 by the country's statistics bureau. Year-on-year inflation in January 2023 was recorded at 27.55 percent, the highest since May 1975, with thousands of containers of imports held up at Karachi port. Pakistan's economy is in dire straits, stricken by a balance-of-payments crisis while it attempts to service high amounts of external debt.

- The United Nations cultural organization, UNESCO, designated the historic center of Odesa as a World Heritage Site and categorized it as being "in danger" during a committee meeting in Paris. It is in recognition of the historical significance of a Black Sea port that Russia has pounded with missiles as it seeks to retake Ukraine.

- Equatorial Guinea has appointed Manuela Roka Botey as prime minister. She became the first woman in the country to hold the position. President Teodoro Obiang Nguema Mbasogo, who has ruled the country since 1979, made the announcement in a decree read on state television.

- Australia announced it will erase the British monarch from its banknotes, replacing the late Queen Elizabeth II's image on its $5 note with a design honoring Indigenous culture. The central bank's decision to leave her successor Charles III off the $5 note means no Britain-based monarch will remain on Australia's paper currency.

- Indian American Congressman Dr. Ami Bera has been appointed as a member of a powerful US House Committee handling intelligence-related matters. The House Permanent Selection Committee on Intelligence is charged with providing oversight of the country's intelligence activities, including the Central Intelligence Agency (CIA), office of the Director of National Intelligence (DNI), National Security Agency (NSA) as well as the military intelligence programs.

- A 7.8 magnitude earthquake shook Turkey followed by another strong quake which was felt in several provinces in the region, knocking down a number of buildings, reports said. The US Geological Survey said quake was centred about 33 kilometres (20 miles) from Gaziantep about 26 kilometres (16 miles) from the town of Nurdagi. It was centred 18 kilometres (11 miles) deep, according to the US Geological Survey. Turkey's Disaster and Emergency Management agency was centred in the town of Pazarcik, in Kahramanmaras province.

- India, France and the United Arab Emirates (UAE) announced the creation of a formal trilateral cooperation initiative for projects in solar and nuclear energy, the fight against climate change and joint production of military hardware. The initiative will also act as a platform to bolster cooperation on sustainable projects between the development agencies of the three countries, which will also work to align their economic, technological and social policies with the objectives of the Paris Agreement, according to a joint statement.

- India and the European Union (EU) announced the formation of three working groups under the 'Trade and Technology Council' that was set up to deepen strategic ties with the trade bloc. India and EU had in April last year agreed to establish a 'Trade and Technology Council', to tackle the challenges at the nexus of trade, trusted technology and security. Such a council is the first for India with any of its partners and second for the EU, following the first one it has set up with the United States (US). According to a current United Nations report, North Korea stole more bitcoin assets in 2022 than any other year and targeted the networks of multinational aerospace and defence industries. Independent sanctions monitors reported to a U.N. Security Council committee that (North Korea) used increasingly sophisticated cyber techniques to access digital networks used in cyber finance and to steal information with potential value, including to its weapons programmes.

- Indian-American student at Harvard Law School, Apsara Iyer has been elected president of the prestigious Harvard Law Review, becoming the first woman from the community to be named to the position in the prestigious publication's 136-year history. She was elected the 137th president of the Harvard Law Review, which was founded in 1887 and is among the oldest student-run legal scholarship publications.

- India delivered fifty buses to Sri Lanka at the Presidential Secretariat premises as Sri Lanka celebrated its 75th Independence Day. High Commissioner of India Gopal Baglay handed over the buses to Sri Lanka's President Ranil Wickremesinghe. Ashok Leyland, the commercial vehicle maker Ashok Leyland had bagged the contract for supplying 500 buses to the Sri Lank Transport Board. The order is a part of a Line of Credit extended by the Export-Import Bank of India, under the Economic Assistance Scheme of the Indian government.

- The 6th Shanghai Cooperation Organization (SCO) Supreme Audit Institutions (SAI) Leaders' Meeting is being hosted by the Comptroller and Auditor General (CAG) of India in Lucknow on 6 February. Comptroller and Auditor General of India, Girish Chandra Murmu led the discussions on the theme 'Integrating Emerging Technologies in Audit'.

- New 'everyday' stamps featuring the image of King Charles III were unveiled for the first time, the latest item in Britain to get a makeover following the death of Queen Elizabeth. From coins and banknotes and to the official royal cypher used by the government, Britain has been slowly introducing replacements featuring the new monarch since his mother's death in September.

- A 13-year-old girl, Natasha Perianayagam won the title of "world's brightest" student. Natasha Perianayagam, an Indian American, was named to the list compiled by the Johns Hopkins Center for Talented Youth in the United States.

- Peru reported the death of 585 sea lions and 55,000 wild birds due to the H5N1 bird flu virus in recent weeks. Following the discovery of 55,000 dead birds in eight protected coastal areas, rangers found the bird flu that killed them had also claimed 585 sea lions in seven protected marine areas, the Sernanp natural areas protection agency said.

- Pakistan's Prime Minister Shahbaz Sharif has approved a deal with the International Monetary Fund (IMF) and all matters over the bailout programme are settled, citing sources. Cash-strapped Pakistan had been due to wrap up talks with the IMF in a bid to unlock stalled funds from a $6.5 billion bailout to ward off economic meltdown.

- The commencement of a public campaign to strengthen cyber security in these four countries has been announced by The Quad, a plurilateral structure made up of India, Australia, Japan, and the US.

- In order to speed up the government's reaction to an ongoing energy crisis, South African President Cyril Ramaphosa proclaimed a state of Disaster. He also promised to designate a minister in his office who will concentrate on increasing the supply of power.

- Ahead of the scheduled coronation ceremony for Britain's King Charles III on 6 May, 2023, the Buckingham Palace released the newly appointed king's official coronation emblem. The coronation emblem features the King's love for nature by joining the flora that symbolize the four nations of the United Kingdom in a single image. The logo, to be used for events over the coronation long weekend in May, features a rose, thistle, daffodil and shamrock - emblems from across the United Kingdom.

- Russian state news agencies reported that India received arms worth around $13 billion from Russia in the past five years. Moreover, New Delhi has further placed orders with Moscow for weapons and military equipment exceeding $10 billion.

- As Cyclone Gabrielle approaches the coast of the nation, residents of Auckland, the largest city in New Zealand, and the surrounding area are being warned to prepare for more intense rain, flooding, and gale-force winds. Some homes are also being evacuated. A former judge and freedom fighter, Mohammad Shahabuddin Chuppu, was elected unopposed as Bangladesh's 22nd President. A gazette was issued on the appointment of the new Bangladesh President by the Chief Election Commissioner.

- Nikos Christodoulides was elected as the President of Cyprus after a second and final round of voting. Christodoulides, 49, took 51.9% of the vote, compared with runoff rival Andreas Mavroyiannis, 66, taking 48.1%. Christodoulides ran as an independent with the backing of centrist and right-of-center parties.

- The first-ever woman astronaut of Saudi Arabia will go to space this year, Saudi woman astronaut Rayyana Barnawi will join fellow Saudi Ali Al-Qarni on a 10-day mission to the International Space Station (ISS) this year. Barnawi and Al-Qarni will fly to the ISS aboard a SpaceX Dragon spacecraft as part of a mission by the private space company Axiom Space.

- The Indian Institute of Technology (IIT) Indore Students won AED 1 million by winning the gold medal at the World Government Summit in Dubai. Niyati Totala and Neel Kalpeshkumar Parikh of The Indian Institute of Technology (IIT) Indore, were awarded the prestigious medal by Egyptian President Abel Fattah AlSisi.

- World Bank chief David Malpass has announced his resignation nearly a year early. He ending a tenure at the head of the development lender that was clouded by questions over his climate stance. The veteran of Republican administrations in the United States was appointed to the role in 2019 when Donald Trump was president and previously served as Under Secretary of the Treasury for international affairs. Malpass's term would have originally ended in 2024.

- Indian-origin Republican leader Nikki Haley formally launched her 2024 presidential bid, casting herself as a younger, fresher alternative to her one-time boss and former US President Donald Trump. Haley, 51, is the two-term Governor of South Carolina and the former US Ambassador to the United Nations.

- The Spanish government approved a historic law granting paid medical leave to women suffering from severe menstrual pain is the first for any European country. These leave facilities are available in a handful of countries including Japan, Indonesia, and Zambia. Equality Minister Irene Montero informed that it is a historic day of progress in feminist rights. In a move to boost the transition to electric vehicles (EVs), the European Parliament has approved the law to ban the sale of new gas and diesel cars in the EU, starting in 2035. The new legislation sets the path towards zero C02 emissions for new passenger cars and light commercial vehicles in 2035.

- Qatar has lifted its temporary ban on the import of frozen seafood from India, paving the way for enhanced export and improved bilateral relations with the West Asian country, the Ministry of Commerce and Industry said in a statement.

- India has been collaborating with numerous countries and organizations to counter global terrorism at various levels. Egypt is one such country with whom India has constantly worked to combat terrorism. The third meeting of the India-Egypt Joint Working Group on Counter Terrorism was conducted on February 16, 2023, in New Delhi.

- Saudi Arabia's Crown Prince unveiled The Mukaab, which is a 400-meter-high, wide, and long long indoor supercity in the center of Riyadh. The Mukaab, the super city, will be large enough to hold 20 empire state buildings and it is aimed that the PIF-backed gigaproject will become a new global icon of technology, sustainability, mobility, and Saudi Innovation.

- Afshan Khan, an Indo-Canadian, has been named the coordinator of the "Scaling Up Nutrition Movement," according to UN Secretary-General António Guterres.

- India and the UAE are celebrating the first anniversary of their Comprehensive Economic Partnership Agreement, signed on February 18, 2022. As part of continued efforts to boost bilateral trade, the UAE India Business Council - UAE

Chapter (UIBC-UC) was launched on February 18, 2023 by the UAE's minister of state for foreign trade Thani bin Ahmed Al Zeyoudi.

- The Seattle City Council passed an ordinance adding caste to the list of protected classes in the city's municipal code, along with groups like race, religion, and gender identity. Seattle created history by becoming the first US city to pass an explicit ban on caste-based discrimination.

- From Washington, US President Joe Biden is nominating former Mastercard Chief Executive Ajay Banga to lead the World Bank, after its current chief David Malpass announced plans to step down early.

- The UN General Assembly approved a nonbinding resolution that calls for Russia to end hostilities in Ukraine and demands the withdrawal of its forces, sending a strong message on the eve of the first anniversary of the invasion that Moscow's aggression must end. - Bhutan has taken a step towards modernising its digital infrastructure. The Himalayan kingdom has just found its first-ever digital citizen. The Bhutan National Digital Identity (NDI) mobile wallet, Royal Highness The Gyalsey (Prince) Jigme Namgyel Wangchuck has become the first digital citizen of Bhutan.

- Pakistan's Finance Minister Ishaq Dar said his country has received $700 million funds from the China Development Bank. The deposit comes as Pakistan has been struggling with its external debt and has barely enough dollars to cover less than three weeks' worth of imports. Finance Minister Ishaq Dar referred to the deposit as a "lifeline" for Pakistan.

- The World Bank announced $2.5 billion in additional grant financing from the U.S. Agency for International Development (USAID) to support Ukraine's budget and maintain essential services.

- Bill Gates has acquired a minority stake in Heineken Holding NV, the controlling shareholder of the world's second-largest brewer, for about $902 million. The Microsoft founder and philanthropist picked up 3.8% of Heineken Holding, according to a filing by the Dutch regulator AFM. He bought 6.65 million shares in Heineken Holding, in his individual capacity, and another 4.18 million shares through the Bill & Melinda Gates Foundation Trust.

- India and Guyana have agreed to cooperate in the oil and gas sector, including long-term crude purchase from the South American country and investment in its upstream sector. Oil minister Hardeep Singh Puri met Guyana president Mohamed Irfaan Ali.

- The Financial Action Task Force (FATF), a global organization that monitors financial crime, suspended Russia's membership after finding that Moscow (Russia)'s conflict in Ukraine breached the FATF's principles.

- Crisis-hit Only a month after the Indian multinational conglomerate's shares crashed as a result of the negative report on the Group by American short-seller Hindenburg, Sri Lanka has accepted a $442 million wind power projects of Adani Green Energy.

- A Russian Soyuz spacecraft launched on a mission to return to Earth a crew who were left stranded on the International Space Station (ISS) due to a cooling system leak in their previous return capsule. According to the Tass news agency, the unmanned Soyuz MS-23 launched from Kazakhstan's Baikonur space centre and was successfully sent into orbit. The ISS was to be docked with it.

- The Afghan embassy in Pakistan's capital, Islamabad, announced the reopening of the Torkham border. Pakistani officials and Afghanistan's Taliban-appointed administrator in Afghanistan's Nangarhar province also confirmed that the border crossing is open to passengers and trade.

- China sent the Zhongxing-26 communications satellite into orbit Feb. 23, marking the resumption orbital launches following a pause for Chinese New Year. A Long March 3B rocket lifted off at 6:49 a.m. Eastern (1149 UTC) from Xichang, southwest China, successfully sending Zhongxing-26 (ChinaSat-26) into geosynchronous transfer orbit (GTO). The China Aerospace Science and Technology Corporation (CASC) confirmed launch success within the hour.

- Amid the severe economic crisis, Pakistan's government has decided to raise the policy rate to 19 per cent or 200 basis points, which will be an increase of 2 per cent. Currently, it stands at 17 per cent.

- The Britain and the European Union(EU) agreed on a new trading arrangement for Northern Ireland, a move aimed at ending years of friction caused by Brexit and allowing greater cooperation between both sides at a time of mounting geo-political risk to Europe from Russia's war in Ukraine.

National Current Affairs

- The President of India Droupadi Murmu addressed the 31st Foundation Day of the National Commission for Women in Delhi on January 31st, 2023. The theme of the program was 'Sashakt Nari Sashakt Bharat' which aimed at acknowledging and celebrating the stories of women who have excelled and paved their journey to leave a mark.

- Going greener and more sustainable towards the environment, the Indian Railways is introducing a green revolution and will be introducing hydrogen and electric trains to the eight heritage routes in the country by December 2023. The Union Minister for Railways Ashwini Vaishnaw confirmed this recently. These hydrogen trains will include the modified version of steam engines, that will be back on tracks, equipped with vintage sirens and green steam vapours.

- India will be invited as the focal country at the Madrid International Book Fair in 2025, the Ambassador of Spain to India, Jose Maria Ridao said. Spain is the theme country at the 46th International Kolkata Book Fair. The Madrid International Book Fair is an annual event held in the Buen Retiro Park in Madrid.

- Minority Affairs Minister Smriti Irani has informed that the Government, under the Annual Bilateral Agreement with Saudi Arabia for Haj pilgrimage this year, has restored the original Haj quota which stands at 1,75,025.

- Minister of Tourism G. Kishan Reddy launched the Visit India Year - 2023 initiative and unveiled the logo in New Delhi. Minister of Tourism G. Kishan Reddy kicked off the year of grand plans and activities for promoting tourism in the country.

- Union Home Minister Amit Shah laid the foundation stone of a ₹450 crore nano urea plant and township of the Indian Farmers Fertiliser Cooperative (IFFCO) in

Deoghar, Jharkhand. The nano urea plant will be the fifth such plant in India. Prime Minister Narendra Modi inaugurated the world's first nano urea plant in Gujarat in 2021. According to Union Minister Amit Shah Nano Urea will benefit farmers and it is already being exported to five countries.

- Prime Minister Narendra Modi inaugurated the India Energy Week (IEW) 2023 event that aimed to showcase India's rising prowess as an energy transition powerhouse. The IEW is being held in Bengaluru from 6th to 8th February 2023. Union Minister for Petroleum and Natural Gas Hardeep Singh Puri, Governor Thaawarchand Gehlot, and CM Basavaraj Bommai also felicitated the event.

- Prime Minister Narendra Modi dedicated the HAL Helicopter Factory to the nation in Tumakuru. He also laid the foundation stone of the Tumakuru Industrial Township and two Jal Jeevan Mission projects at Tiptur and Chikkanayakanahalli in Tumakuru. The Prime Minister took a walkthrough of the Helicopter Facility and Structure Hangar and unveiled the Light Utility Helicopter.

- Vice President Jagdeep Dhankhar inaugurated the 36th Surajkund International Crafts Mela at Faridabad, Haryana. On the inaugural occasion, he urged everyone to consider locally produced handicraft items when looking for gifts for their friends and relatives. He underscored that such an approach would not only help in the conservation of many unique art forms but also enhance the economic condition of the talented artisans & craftsmen.

- Reliance Jio in collaboration with GSMA has unveiled a nationwide Digital Skill initiative. This collaborative effort intends to provide rural women and people from low-income groups with training based on their specific needs.

- The Yuva Sangam registration portal was launched in New Delhi. The Yuva Sangam is an initiative of Prime Minister Narendra Modi to build close ties between the youth of the Northeast Region and the rest of India under the spirit of Ek Bharat Shreshtha Bharat. Under the initiative, over 20 thousand youth will travel across the country and gain a unique opportunity for crosscultural learning. Union Minister of Ayush Sarbananda Sonowal and Union Minister of Health and Family Welfare Dr. Mansukh Mandaviya jointly inaugurated the Integrative Medicine Centre at Safdarjung Hospital. Minister of State for Health, Dr. Bharati Pravin Pawar, and

Minister of State for Ayush, Dr. Munjapara Mahendrabhai Kalubhai, and Secretary Ayush, Vaidya Rajesh Kotecha were also present on the occasion.

- Prime Minister Narendra Modi inaugurated the Aljamea-tus-Saifiyah, Arabic Academy of the Dawoodi Bohra Community in Mumbai. The Prime minister was accompanied by His Holiness Syedna Mufaddal Saifuddin, the 53rd al-Dai al-Mutlaq, head of the global Dawoodi Bohra community and Rector of Jamea, Eknath Sindhe, Chief Minister of Maharashtra and deputy Chief Minister Devendra Fadnavis.

- Prime Minister Narendra Modi flagged off two new Vande Bharat Trains from Chhatrapati Shivaji Maharaj Terminus. The new and upgraded version of Vande Bharat Express will connect Mumbai and Solapur and Mumbai and Sainagar Shirdi. Mumbai-Solapur train, the ninth Vande Bharat Train will connect the country's commercial capital to the City of Textiles and Hutatmas in Maharashtra.

- Meta, announced its partnership with the ministry of electronics and information technology (MeitY) for the G20 stay safe online campaign. As part of the partnership, the company claims that it will create and share helpful resources in multiple Indian languages through various channels, and spread awareness on how to stay safe online. Moreover, Meta has also launched its #DigitalSuraksha campaign to build on the company's efforts to offer a safer and more inclusive internet to everyone.

- Prime Minister Narendra Modi inaugurated the 14th edition of its flagship aero show in Bengaluru, an event seen to be a great business opportunity when New Delhi is looking to push indigenous products, modernise Soviet-era equipment and as domestic carriers add fleet. The theme of Aero India 2023 is "The Runway to a Billion Opportunities".

- The Minister for Communications, Electronics & Information Technology and Railways, Ashwini Vaishnaw inaugurated AMRITPEX 2023 - National Philatelic Exhibition. This five-day Mahakumbh of Stamps is being celebrated from 11th February to 15th February 2023 and is being organized as a part of Azadi Ka Amrit Mahotsav Celebrations.

- Prime Minister Narendra Modi celebrated the 200th birth Anniversary of Maharishi Dayanand Saraswati, who founded the Arya Samaj in 1875. According to Prime Minister Narendra Modi, the nation is making development thanks to non-discriminatory efforts and policies. The first yagya for the nation, he claimed, is being performed today in service of the poor, uneducated, and oppressed. In this regard, Mr. Modi emphasised housing, healthcare, and women's empowerment.
- India's first air-conditioned double-decker electric bus was inducted into the fleet of BEST- the civic transport public body in Mumbai. The wet-leased e-bus will be registered at the Regional Transport Office before it hits the road for the public. This air-conditioned doubledecker electric bus is likely to ply on the routes in suburbs where conventional double-decker buses that run on diesel are currently operated.

- Prime Minister Narendra Modi inaugurated the National Aadi Mahotsav on 16th February 2023 at Major Dhyan Chand National Stadium, New Delhi. This was announced at a media briefing by the Union Minister of Tribal Affairs, Arjun Munda in New Delhi.

- Union Environment Minister Bhupender Yadav announced Twelve cheetahs will be flown in from South Africa on 18th February. Under the ambitious Cheetah reintroduction program, Prime Minister Narendra Modi released the first batch of eight spotted felines -five females and three males -- from Namibia into a quarantine enclosure at the Kuno National Park in Madhya Pradesh on his 72nd birthday on September 17 last year.

- Prime Minister Narendra Modi inaugurated the National Aadi Mahotsav on 16th February 2023 at Major Dhyan Chand National Stadium, New Delhi. This was announced at a media briefing by the Union Minister of Tribal Affairs, Arjun Munda in New Delhi. Minister of State for Tribal Affairs, Renuka Saruta was also present on the occasion. Arjun Munda also informed that the Prime Minister will be given an overview of the products which will be on display at various stalls and will engage with the artisans and the craftsmen from the tribal communities.

- Prime Minister Narendra Modi inaugurated the Jal Jan Abhiyan virtually on Abu Road in the Sirohi district of Rajasthan. PM Modi noted that the 21st-century world is realizing the seriousness of limited water resources on earth and pointed out that water security is a huge question for India due to its large population. He informed that in the Amrit Kaal, India is looking towards the water as the future.

- The Union Cabinet approved the signing of the memorandum of understanding (MoU) between the India and Republic of South Africa for cooperation in the 'disability sector'. The Ministry of Social Justice and Empowerment said that the bilateral MoU would encourage cooperation between the Department of Empowerment of Persons with Disabilities, the Government of India and South Africa through joint initiatives in the disability sector.

- The Union Cabinet approved signing of a Memorandum of Understanding (MoU) between India and Chile for cooperation in the field of agriculture and allied sectors. The MoU will come in force upon its signature and will remain effective for 5 years from the date of execution after which it will be automatically renewed for another 5 years.

- The Unique Identification Authority of India (UIDAI) has recently launched a chatbot to help people get an answer to their queries related to the Aadhaar card. It is called "Aadhaar Mitra". The Artificial Intelligence/Machine Learning (AI/ML)-a based chatbot can answer queries related to Aadhaar enrolment number, PVC Card order status, and complaint status, among other things. It is available in both English and Hindi languages.

- External Affairs Minister S Jaishankar unveiled Sardar Vallabhbhai Patel's bust in India House in Suva and interacted with a large gathering of members of the diaspora community. S. Jaishankar informed that he was privileged to unveil a bust of Sardar Patel at the India House in Suva, Fiji. His vision of a united, stronger nation remains an inspiration for all Indians.

- Advancing India's cyber-preparedness, KAVACH-2023, a national level hackathon was launched to identify innovative ideas and technological solutions for addressing the cyber security and cybercrime challenges of the 21st century. KAVACH-2023 is a one-of-a-kind national hackathon jointly developed by All India Council for Technical Education (AICTE), Bureau of Police Research and Development (BPRD) and Indian Cyber Crime Coordination Centre.

- A memorandum of understanding (MoU) was signed by Rolls-Royce Marine North America and Kalyani Strategic Service Limited (KSSL), a 100% subsidiary of Bharat Forge, to investigate the possibility of KSSL serving as an in-country provider for propeller sales in the Indian market.

- The Centre banned two groups and declared an individual a terrorist for their subversive and anti-India activities. The two groups are the Jammu and Kashmir Ghaznavi Force (JKGF), which has been formed with cadres from terrorist organisations such as the Lashkare-Taiba and Jaish-e-Mohammed; and the Khalistan Tiger Force (KTF), which aims to revive terrorism in Punjab.

- The first nuclear power plant in North India would be built in Gorakhpur, Haryana, according to Union Minister Jitendra Singh. According to Singh, the Center has unanimously approved the installation of 10 nuclear reactors in an effort to boost India's nuclear capability.

- Agricultural and Process Food Export Development Authority (APEDA) is participating in the 28th edition of Gulfood 2023 which will be held in UAE. India has been participating in GULFOOD which is a platform that connects food and beverage sectors around the globe, providing ample opportunities to Indian exporters.

- The Union cabinet, chaired by Prime Minister Narendra Modi, on February 22 extended the term of the 22 nd Law Commission till August 31, 2024. The move came as the tenure of the 22nd Law Commission of India ended on February 20, 2023.

- Biodiversity, the totality and variety of our biological resources, is crucial to the survival of the world. The United Nations Biodiversity Conference in Montreal, Canada, made a strong case for the value of our planet's biodiversity. The 2030 commitment, which aims to "stop and reverse" biodiversity loss by protecting 30% of the world's land and 30% of its oceans by 2030 , was ratified on December 19, 2022, by delegates from 188 nations. India is in a prime position to lead the world in becoming biodiversity champions because it currently has 17% of the world's population and 17% of the world's biodiversity hotspots.

- According to the Election Commission of India (ECI), more than 60% of India's 94.5 crore voters have connected their Aadhaar numbers to their voter IDs. There are 56,90,83,090 voters who are linked to their Aadhaar overall.

- Prime Minister Narendra Modi inaugurated the 'Barisu Kannada Dim Dimava cultural festival at Talkatora Stadium in Delhi on 25th February 2023. Prime Minister Modi addressed the gathering on the occasion.

- The Chief Justice of India DY Chandrachud announced that the Supreme Court has launched "neutral citations" of judgments to ensure a uniform pattern of citing its decisions.

- Union Home Minister and Minister of Cooperation, Amit Shah addressed the 'Kol Janjati Mahakumbh' organized on the occasion of Shabri Mata Janm Jayanti at Satna, Madhya Pradesh.

- Chief Minister Eknath Shinde confirmed that Aurangabad city will be renamed Chhatrapati Sambhajinagar, and Osmanabad city will be called Dharashiv. After a year the proposal to rename Aurangabad and Osmanabad has been approved by the Ministry of Home Affairs.

States Current Affairs

- Visakhapatnam, a port and industrial city brimming with cosmopolitan culture has been in the news ever since Andhra Pradesh Chief Minister YS Jagan Mohan Reddy's government announced that it would be the new capital of the state, indicating plans to develop Amaravati - on the banks of the Krishna river - as the capital city have been scrapped. The announcement of Visakhapatnam, a new capital for Andhra comes nine years after the state of Telangana was carved out of its territory and given Hyderabad as its capital.

- The Uttar Pradesh government has launched a campaign to empower girls from the underprivileged class. The Samagra Shiksha Abhiyan will work under the Aarohini Initiative Training Programme for the safety and security of girls in 746 Kasturba Gandhi Residential Girls Schools in Uttar Pradesh.

- The Government of Goa has launched the Vision for All School Eye Health program in partnership with OneSight EssilorLuxottica Foundation and Prasad Netralaya. The program is an extension of the current Vision for All Goa eye health program.
- The Maharashtra government announced the Jai Jai Maharashtra Majha as the state song, which is usually performed at school cultural events on May 1, second only to the national anthem. The song will now be played on official occasions. The national anthem will always take precedence, and the state song will play at all government-organised events, according to rules established by the state cabinet.

- The Madhya Pradesh government announced that Islam Nagar village, situated in the Bhopal district, has been renamed as Jagdishpur. The MP administration, in an official release, declared the changes and mentioned the change in the name with immediate effect.

- Nagaland government has signed a Memorandum of Understanding (MoU) with Patanjali Foods Limited for development and area expansion under palm oil cultivation and processing for Zone-II (Mokokchung, Longleng, and Mon districts) of Nagaland under the National Mission on Edible Oils-Oil Palm (NMEO-OP).

- The Delhi Commission for Protection of Child Rights (DCPCR) unveiled "Bal Mitra," a WhatsApp chatbot designed to improve communication between kids and parents in Delhi. "The chatbot 'Bal Mitra' will serve as a source of reliable information regarding children and their rights," claims Manish Sisodia, the deputy chief minister of Delhi.

- The Kerala government announced a scheme of Rs 200 crore for developing green hydrogen hubs at Trivandrum and Kochi. Kerala aims to become a 100 percent renewable energy-dependent state by 2040 and a net carbon-neutral state by 2050 . The state has a favorable atmosphere for the production of green hydrogen.

- The Kala Ghoda Arts Festival began on 4th February and will go on till 12th February 2023. The Kala Ghoda Arts Festival is Asia's biggest multicultural festival. The festival is happening after a break of two years due to the Covid-19 pandemic.

- Himachal Chief Minister Sukhvinder Singh Sukhu laid the foundation stone of 'Himachal Niketan' which will provide accommodation facilities to the students and residents of Himachal Pradesh visiting New Delhi. 'Himachal Niketan', a five-story building will be constructed in Dwarka, Delhi for Rs. 57.72 crore.

- The Uttar Pradesh government has launched the portal for the creation of 'Family ID - One Family One Identity', to identify families as a unit for implementing the 'one job per family' proposal. According to a state government, all such families that are not eligible for the National Food Security Scheme will be able to avail of the ID, while the ration card ID of the families having it, will be considered as their family ID.

- The country's strictest Anti-Copying Law has come into force in Uttarakhand. Governor Lieutenant General Gurmeet Singh has approved the Uttarakhand Competitive Examination (Measures for Prevention and Prevention of Unfair Means in Recruitment) Ordinance 2023. In view of this, the Anti-Copying Law is being described as the biggest anti-copying law in the country. This comes after the UKPSC paper leak which led to cancellation of exam for around 1.4 lakh government job aspirants.

- Union Minister of Chemicals and Fertilizers, Dr. Mansukh Mandaviya inaugurated the IFFCO Nano Urea Liquid Plants at Aonla and Phulpur in Uttar Pradesh. Dr. Mandaviya stated that it is an important day because Nano urea plants have been dedicated to the nation. He informed that Nano Urea, in the coming times will ensure the progress of the farmers and increase their income.

- The state government of Maharashtra has announced that renowned social worker, preacher and reformer Dattatreya alias Appasaheb Dharmadikari will be honoured with Maharashtra Bhushan award for the year 2022. The Maharashtra Bhushan award comprises a medal, a citation and Rs 25 lakh, which will be conferred to Appasaheb at a function later in the year. Appasaheb was honoured with Padmashri in 2017.

- Union Home Minister Amit Shah has presented the President's Colour to Haryana Police in recognition of its exceptional service. He Shah presented the award on behalf of President Dedroupadi Murmu in a ceremony at the Haryana Police

Academy in Karnal's Madhuban. In his remarks at the event, Shah also paid tribute to those martyred in the 2019 Pulwama attack. He added that the names of the 40 Central Reserve Police Force personnel who died would be written in "golden letters" in India's defence history.

- Punjab Government has organized its first state-level 'Prawn Fair' (Shrimp mela). This "Prawn Fair" or Shrimp mela is an effort of the state government to create awareness about shrimp farming.

- Union Minister for Road Transport and Highways Nitin Gadkari laid the Foundation Stone of the world's largest and unique Divyang Park - Anubhuti Inclusive Park in Nagpur, Maharashtra. On the occasion, he informed that the park is being developed keeping in mind the vision of Prime Minister Narendra Modi to build an inclusive society. Instead of sympathy, this park will show empathy, hence this park has been named Anubhuti Divyang Park.

- The seven-day 49th Khajuraho Dance Festival will begin with Bharatnatyam and kathak at the temple declared as UNESCO heritage. The annual event of the Khajuraho Dance Festival is being organized by Ustad Allauddin Khan Sangeet Evam Kala Akademi and the directorate of culture in association with the tourism department and the Archaeological Survey of India.

- Statehood Day in Arunachal Pradesh is a state holiday observed on 20th February in the Northeastern Indian state of Arunachal Pradesh. Statehood Day in Arunachal Pradesh is celebrated to commemorate the granting of statehood to the state which occurred in the year 1987.

- The Taj Mahotsav was officially launched on February 20 in Agra by Yogendra Upadhyay, minister of higher education for the state of Uttar Pradesh. He claimed that the 10-day festival had drawn tourists from other countries in addition to locals. A total of 300 artisans from a number of states and UTs, including Jammu & Kashmir, West Bengal, Bihar, and Himachal Pradesh, are taking part in the event this year, which has as its subject "Vishwa Bandhutva."

- Governor of Odisha Prof. Ganeshi Lal launched India's first AI Chatbot for the Agricultural sector 'Ama KrushAI' at the valedictory session of 'Krushi Odisha 2023'. Ama KrushAI chatbot will help the farmers with the best agronomic practices, inform them about government schemes, and loan products from more than 40 commercial and cooperative banks.

- The first Prime Minister GatiShakti regional workshop for the Western and Central Zone was held in Goa. The workshop featured discussions on use cases of National Master Plan (NMP) adoption by Central Ministries & State Departments for planning and acted as a platform for mutual learning among the States and Central Ministries/Departments.

- The Election Commission recognized the faction led by Maharashtra Chief Minister Eknath Shinde as the real Shiv Sena and allocated it the bow and arrow symbol. In the order, the Election Commission informed that 40 MLAs backing Shinde got nearly 76% of the votes polled in favor of the 55 Shiv Sena candidates who had won their seats in the 2019 Maharashtra Assembly polls.

- Eknath Shinde, the chief minister of Maharashtra, was elected as the Shiv Sena's supreme leader during the party's national executive meeting. The Election Commission of India (ECI) recognised his faction as the true Shiv Sena and gave him the "bow and arrow" insignia during the first national executive meeting following that recognition. The MLAs, MPs, and other Sena leaders who had joined Shinde after he split from the group headed by former chief minister Uddhav Thackeray were present at the meeting.

- On February 21, also known as International Mother Language Day, the Kerala High Court published two of its most recent decisions in Malayalam, making it the first high court in the nation to do so.

- The Churchgate railway station in Mumbai will soon be called as 'Chintamanrao Deshmukh station', named after the first governor of the Reserve Bank of India (RBI) CD Deshmukh.

- Gujarat Legislative Assembly has unanimously passed a Bill that provides for up to 10 years in prison to curb paper leaks in government recruitment exams. According to the provisions of the bill, the accused shall also be liable for a fine which shall not be less than Rs 10 lakh, which may extend to Rs 1 crore.

- The Uttarakhand government has signed a contract to construct a 3.38 km ropeway from Janki Chatti in Kharsali to Yamunotri Dham. To be built at a cost of Rs 166.82 crore, the ropeway will cut down the travel time from the current 2-3 hours to just 20 minutes.

- The Kerala government has launched robotic scavenger, "Bandicoot", to clean sewages in the temple town of Guruvayur, becoming the first state in the country to use robotic technology to clean all its commissioned manholes. Water Resources Minister Roshi Augustine, launched Bandicoot under the Guruvayur Sewerage Project in Thrissur district by the Kerala Water Authority (KWA), as part of the 100-day action plan of the state government.

- The Kerala government and UN Women entered into an agreement, in order to promote activities that are welcoming to women in the State's tourist industry. Kerala Tourism and UN Women India committed to promoting gender-inclusive tourist destinations throughout the State through the signing of a memorandum of understanding (MoU).

- The Karnataka Government will build the country's first Marina or a boat basin offering dockage, at Byndoor in Udupi district to promote coastal tourism in Karnataka. The government will also seek permission from the Centre for the relaxation of coastal regulation zone (CRZ) to take up beach tourism in coastal areas and pilgrim tourism.

- Japan's eminent hospitality group Hotel Management International Company Limited (HMI) will be opening 30 new properties across Uttar Pradesh. The company has signed an MoU with the UP government to invest Rs 7200 crore at the UP Global Investors Summit.

- The foundation stone-laying ceremony for the first-ever compressed biogas plant project in northeast India took place at Domora Pathar in Sonapur under the Kamrup (Metropolitan) district, and the chief guest was chief minister Himanta Biswa Sarma.

Schemes/Committees

- The Shipping Ministry has formed a committee to draft revised Guidelines for operationalization of Roll on-Roll off (Ro-Ro) and Roll on-Passenger (Ro-Pax) ferry service. This committee, headed by the Chairman, Deendayal Port Authority, would also draft the Model Concession Agreement for Ro-Ro or Ro-Pax Terminal Operator and Model License Agreement for Operation of the ferry services in the country.

- Namami Gange Programme was launched from June 2014 till 31st March 2021 to rejuvenate River Ganga and its tributaries with a budget of Rs. 20,000 crore. The Government of India has approved Namami Gange Mission-II with a budgetary outlay of Rs. 22,500 crore till 2026 including projects for existing liabilities (Rs.11,225 Cr) and new projects/interventions (Rs.11,275 crore).

- The Ministry of Tourism under its schemes of 'Swadesh Darshan' and 'National Mission on Pilgrimage Rejuvenation and Spiritual, Heritage Augmentation Drive (PRASHAD)' has identified four pilgrim centers for development. They provide financial assistance to State Governments/UT Administrations etc. for the development of tourism infrastructure in the country.

- The deadline for completing projects under the Smart Cities Mission (SCM) was extended for all 100 participating cities to June 2023 due to the delays caused by COVID-19 and based on a NITI Aayog recommendation, according to Housing and Urban Affairs Ministry. In response to several questions about Smart City projects in the country, the Ministry informed the Lok Sabha that "the period of implementation of SCM has been extended to June 2023".

- The Cabinet approved the 'Vibrant Villages Programme' to ensure the comprehensive development of villages along the northern border areas. Out of the financial allocation of Rs 4,800 crore, Rs 2,500 crore would be used for constructing roads. To improve the quality of life and encourage people to stay in their native locations in border areas, the union government announced a Rs 4,800 crore centrally sponsored scheme for four years through FY26.

- The government said it has set up a committee to monitor the impact of rise in temperature on the wheat crop. The move comes amid a forecast by the National Crop Forecast Centre (NCFC) that maximum temperature in major wheat producing areas barring Madhya Pradesh was higher-than-average of the last seven years during the first week of February. Even the Met Department has projected above-normal temperature in Gujarat, Jammu, Himachal Pradesh and Uttarakhand, in next two days. Cabinet Secretary Rajiv Gauba will head a top panel comprising a senior official from the Prime Minister's Office, seven secretaries, among others, to monitor the implementation of the government's ambitious Mission Karmayogi programme for training of government employees.

- Power Minister RK Singh launched South Asia Distribution Utility Network (SADUN) which aims to modernise distribution of utilities in South Asia via knowledge sharing among discoms. SADUN is a joint initiative of the Ministry of Power, USAID and PFC. Singh said that all the member nations would benefit from the synergy, exchange of experiences and the sharing of vision-enabled by the network.

- The Minister of State for Statistics and Programme Implementation, Rao Inderjit Singh, launched the revised norms for MPLADS (Members of Parliament Local Area Development Scheme). He also launched a new Web Portal for the Revised Fund Flow Procedure under MPLADS.

- The Pradhan Mantri Kisan Samman Nidhi Yojana (PM-KISAN) completed 4 years on 24 February 2023. It Pradhan Mantri Kisan Samman Nidhi Yojana or PMKISAN Yojana was launched by Prime Minister Narendra Modi on 24 February 2019 to meet the financial needs of land-holding farmers.

- The Centre said that around 39 crore loans have been extended under Pradhan Mantri Mudra Yojana till 27th of January 2023. The scheme was introduced in 2015.

- Prime Minister Narendra Modi disburse the 13th installment of the income support programme PM-Kisan, totaling more than Rs 16,800 crore to more than eight crore beneficiary farmers in Belagavi, Karnataka.

- D2C(Direct to Consumer) personal care brand Pilgrim has announced its first-ever ESOP scheme. It has earmarked 10% of its shares to the ESOP pool for 100% of its employees, it said in a statement. About 30 employees who have spent a year in the company will be able to benefit from this scheme. With this announcement, Pilgrim aims to acknowledge and reward the efforts of the employees who've led the brand's growth over the last 3.5 years, along with driving wealth creation.

- India has joined a global initiative started by the US and the UAE to boost funding and assistance for the development of climate-smart agriculture and food systems. The two countries together launched the Agricultural Innovation Mission for Climate (AIM4C) in November 2021.

Agreement/Memorandum of Understanding (MoU)

- Reliance Consumer Products Limited, the FMCG firm and a wholly-owned subsidiary of Reliance Retail Ventures Limited announced a strategic partnership with Sri Lanka-headquartered Maliban Biscuit Manufactories Limited. Maliban, a biscuit manufacturer, has been well-known for the last 70 years for its range of quality products including biscuits, crackers, cookies, and wafers. According to the partnership, the company has expanded its product's reach to global markets and exports to over 35 countries across five continents.

- India has welcomed Congo to International Solar Alliance. The External Affairs Ministry said Ambassador of Republic of Congo, Raymond Serge Bale signed the International Solar Alliance Framework Agreement in the presence of Joint Secretary.

- Energy Efficiency Services (EESL), a joint venture of public sector undertakings under the Ministry of Power, signed a Memorandum of Understanding (MoU) with Indonesia-Malaysia-Thailand Growth Triangle Joint Business Council (IMT-GT JBC) Malaysia at India Energy Week (IEW). The MoU aims to promote the adoption of energy efficiency and sustainable practices in the region.

- The Directorate General of GST Intelligence (DGGI) and the National Forensic Sciences University (NFSU) signed a Memorandum of Understanding (MoU) for setting up digital forensic laboratories along with the exchange of information and knowledge, technological advancement and skill development in the field of digital forensics.

- Samsung Semiconductor India Research (SSIR) has announced a new partnership with the Indian Institute of Science (IISc) to promote research and development in the field of on-chip Electrostatic Discharge (ESD) Protection. Samsung India announced that it will hire around 1000 engineers for its R&D institutes, including its Samsung Semiconductor India Research in Bengaluru last year.

- Air India Ltd. has signed deals with Airbus SE and Boeing Co. for what may end up being the largest acquisition of aircraft in commercial aviation history. In an effort to rebuild itself with a fleet that can compete with regional low-cost rivals and strong Gulf airlines like Emirates.

- India and Fiji have signed a pact to exempt visas for holders of diplomatic and official passports. As of now, India has diplomatic and official passport holders' visa exemption pacts with 59 other countries as per the PassportIndia.gov.in website.

- Prime Minister Narendra Modi had a telephone conversation with Spanish PM Pedro Sánchez and both leaders agreed to collaborate on issues such as digital infrastructure, climate action, clean energy transition and sustainable development. Prime Minister's Office (PMO) in a statement said that the leaders discussed a number of bilateral and international issues of mutual interest.

- The Central Water Commission (CWC), Department of Water Resources, River Development & Ganga Rejuvenation, Ministry of Jal Shakti entered into a Memorandum of Agreement for Development of International Centre of Excellence for Dams (ICED) under externally funded Dam Rehabilitation and Improvement Project Phase II and Phase III. This MoA will remain valid for ten years or till the duration of the DRIP Phase-II and Phase-II Scheme, whichever is earlier, from the date of signing.

- The Union Cabinet, chaired by the Hon'ble Prime Minister Shri Narendra Modi, has approved the signing of Memorandum of Understanding between the Institute of Chartered Accountants of India (ICAI) and The Institute of Chartered Accountants in England & Wales (ICAEW). The MoU is to provide recognition of the qualification, training of each other's members and admit the members in good standing by prescribing a bridging mechanism on the prevailing terms and conditions.

- Ministry of Rural Development signed an MoU between the ministry and Meesho an e-commerce platform owned by Bengaluru-based Fashnear Technologies Private Limited. As per the agreement, the e-commerce platform will help in the marketing of products made by the Self-Help Groups under the Deendayal Antyodaya Yojana - National Rural Livelihood Mission.

- Navratna Defence PSU Bharat Electronics Ltd (BEL) said, it signed a Memorandum of Understanding with Aeronautical Development Agency (ADA), DRDO, for the Advanced Medium Combat Aircraft (AMCA) programme.

- Waipapa Taumata Rau, University of Auckland, New Zealand, and Tata Memorial Hospital (TMH), Mumbai, the largest and the most renowned cancer care hospital and research centre in India, have signed a Memorandum of Understanding (MoU) to engage in long-term cooperation in cancer care.

- Hindustan Aeronautics (HAL), an aerospace company in India, and EDGE, the top defence company in the UAE, inked a Memorandum of Understanding at the International Defense Exhibition and Conference (IDEX). The Memorandum of Understanding is signed to examine potential areas of collaboration, such as collaborative development of missile systems and unmanned aerial vehicles (drones).

Appointments/Resignations (National & International)

- Sports brand Puma India announced roping in women's cricket team captain Harmanpreet Kaur as its latest brand ambassador. As part of the partnership terms, Harmanpreet will endorse the brand's footwear, apparel and accessories throughout the year.

- Morgan Stanley named Arun Kohli as the new India head to replace Sanjay Shah, a veteran of 26 years at the firm, who is retiring. Kohli, currently the chief operating officer for EMEA, will head the US bank's business in the country, according to a memo seen by Bloomberg News. With the bank since 2007, Kohli will relocate to Mumbai from London where he headed the firm's post-Brexit strategy and implemented growth strategies across markets in the region.

- Madhvendra Singh appointed as the first Chief Executive Officer (CEO) of Gujarat Ports Infrastructure Company Limited of the Gujarat Maritime Cluster. The Gujarat Maritime Cluster (GMC) is the first of its kind Commercial Maritime Cluster in the country aimed at creating a hub for maritime services of international standards.

- Mahindra Finance has appointed Raul Rebello as Managing Director and Chief Executive Officer Designate. Mahindra Finance is the vehicle financing unit of the Mahindra & Mahindra Group. Raul Rebello is currently the Chief Operating Officer of the company and will take charge as MD and CEO when Ramesh Iyer retires on 29th April 2024.

- Economics professor and researcher Shamika Ravi has been appointed as a member of the Economic Advisory Council to Prime Minister (EAC-PM). She is currently non-resident senior fellow of the governance studies program at the Brookings Institution Washington D.C.

- The Nepal Cricket Association has appointed former Indian cricketer Monty Desai as the head coach of the Nepal national cricket team. He will replace another former Indian cricketer Manoj Prabhakar, who resigned from his post in December 2022. Nepal Cricket Association has signed a two-year deal with Monty Desai.

- The Union Government has appointed K Satyanarayana Raju as its Managing Director and CEO of Canara Bank, with immediate effect. He will be replacing L V Prabhakar who demitted office on December 31, 2022.

- India's Supreme Court is now back to its full strength of 34, with the elevation of two High Court Chief Justices to the apex court. The last time the apex court was at its full strength was in September-November 2019. The Chief Justices of the Allahabad High Court and the Gujarat High Court are the latest additions to the 34judge collegium.

- The Council of the Institute of Chartered Accountants of India (ICAI) elected its new president and vice president. For the 2023-24 term, Aniket Sunil Talati will serve as the president of ICAI, while Ranjeet Kumar Agarwal will be the accounting body's vice president. At the helm of the ICAI's council, Talati and Agarwal will be responsible for organising the three-tiered CA exam and looking after all administrative affairs.

- An Indian-American, Neal Mohan will become the next Chief Executive Officer (CEO) of Alphabet-owned YouTube following Susan Wojcicki's announcement that she will be stepping down from her role as the head of the video-sharing platform.

- Lt Gen MV Suchindra Kumar has been named as the new Vice Chief of Army Staff, while incumbent Lt Gen B S Raju will take charge as South Western Army Commander. Lt Gen Kumar has been promoted as Army Commander and appointed as the new Vice Chief of Army Staff. He is serving as the Deputy Chief of Army Staff (Strategy) in the Army Headquarters at present.

- BCCI's Chief selector Chetan Sharma has resigned from his post following a sting operation conducted by a TV news channel, where he shared internal information about the team and selection process. Chetan Sharma sent his resignation to BCCI Secretary Jay Shah who accepted it.

- Tata Motors, has been appointed Rajan Amba as the Managing Director of Jaguar Land Rover India. He will take charge on March 1, 2023. Amba replaces Rohit Suri, who announced his retirement earlier this year.

- In India, Ayushmann Khurrana will represent UNICEF (United Nations International Children's Emergency Fund). The actor's designation as the National Ambassador was announced by UNICEF.

- Ruchira Kamboj, India's permanent representative to the UN, has been chosen to serve as the commission's chair during the 62nd session. At the opening session of the 62nd session of the UN Commission for Social Development this week in New York, Kamboj was chosen as chair by acclamation.

- One of the major teaching hospitals in the UK, Oxford University Hospitals NHS Foundation Trust, has named Professor Meghana Pandit, a renowned physician of Indian descent, as its CEO.

- Rajeev Singh Raghuvanshi has been appointed as the new Drug Controller General of India (DCGI), Central Drugs Standard Control Organization (CDSCO). Rajeev Singh Raghuvanshi is a former Indian Pharmacopoeia Commission secretary-cum-scientific director.

- The International Labour Organization (ILO), Geneva has chosen the Comptroller and Auditor General of India (CAG) to serve as its external auditor for a four-year term from 2024 to 2027, the apex auditor announced. The CAG is Girish Chandra Murmu.

- Former IAS officer BVR Subrahmanyam was appointed as the new Chief Executive Officer of Niti Aayog. The former Commerce Secretary takes over from Parameswaran lyer, who has been named as the Executive Director of World Bank.

- Lt Gen RS Reen took over as Director General Quality Assurance. A 1986-batch officer, Lt Gen Reen is an alumnus of Indian Military Academy, Dehradun.

Ranks and Reports

- According to the latest Indian Institutional Ranking Framework (IIRF) ranking (2023), the Indian Institute of Management (IIM), Ahmedabad (Gujarat), is the top government college in India for pursuing the Master of Business Administration (MBA) course. IIM Bengaluru (Karnataka) and IIM Kolkata (West Bengal) are ranked second and third, respectively, after IIM Ahmedabad.

- PM Narendra Modi has been pegged as the world's most popular leader with an approval rating of 78 per cent as per a survey by a US-based consulting firm 'Morning Consult.' As per the rating PM Modi's ratings trump those of other leaders including US President Joe Biden, French President Emmanuel Macron and UK Prime Minister Rishi Sunak. The poll surveyed 22 global leaders for the ratings. Neither Vladimir Putin nor Xi Jinping figured among the 22 popular leaders globally.

- Tata Consultancy Services (TCS) has been named to FORTUNE® magazine's list of the World's Most Admired Companies. Regarded as a barometer of corporate reputation, the list is based on a survey of business executives, directors and analysts around the globe.

- Union Minister of Fisheries, Animal Husbandry and Dairying, Parshottam Rupala told Lok Sabha that India is the highest milk producer in the world contributing twenty-four per cent of global milk production in the year 2021-22. According to production data of Food and Agriculture Organization Corporate Statistical Database (FAOSTAT), India is the highest milk producer in the world contributing twenty-four per cent of global milk production in the year 2021-22.

- India's national accreditation system under the Quality Council of India (QCI) has been ranked 5th in the world in the recent Global Quality Infrastructure Index (GQII) 2021. The GQII ranks the 184 economies in the world on the basis of the quality infrastructure (QI).

- India's aviation safety oversight ranking has jumped to the 55th position from 112th place earlier, with a significant improvement in the country's score under the ICAO's coordinated validation mission, according to regulator DGCA.

- Argentina's Lionel Messi is the highest paid athlete in 2021-22 with a total earning of $130 million, a data compiled by Genuine Impact Newsletter. The Argentine star player earned $75 million from on-field through salary and competition winnings, while rest $55 million are from off-field that comes from sponsors, endorsements and non-sporting ventures, etc.

- Among the big States in the country, Chhattisgarh and Bihar allocated the most proportion of their budget towards education in FY23. While Chhattisgarh allocated 18.82 per cent of the State's estimated net budget expenditure to education, Bihar allocated 18.3 per cent.

- Asia will use half of the world's electricity for the first time by 2025 , even as Africa continues to consume far less than its share of the global population, according to a new forecast released by the International Energy Agency. Most of Asia's electricity use will be in China. It is a country with 1.4 billion people whose share of global consumption will rise from a quarter in 2015 to a third by the middle of this decade.

- Mumbai has been ranked as the most-polluted city in India and second most polluted city globally within a week between January 29 and February 8, according to Swiss air tracking index IQAir, a real-time air quality monitor. On February 13, Mumbai took over Delhi as the most polluted city in India and was the third most unhealthy city worldwide for air quality worldwide.

- According to HedgewithCrypto research, India emerged as 7th biggest nation ready to adopt crypto in 2023. Australia is the biggest country when it comes to the adoption of cryptocurrency in 2023 with a score of 7.37 out of 10 . The sale of cryptocurrency and other digital assets is legal and regulated in Australia. Following this, USA ranks as the second biggest country in crypto adoption with a score of 7.07 out of 10 . Currently, there 33,630 crypto ATMs throughout the country.

- India has ranked 42nd among 55 leading global economies on the International IP Index released by the U.S. Chambers of Commerce. The United States ranks first in the 2023 index, followed by the UK and France.

Sports Current Affairs

- Gymnast Dipa Karmakar has been handed a 21-month ban for failing a dope test conducted by the International Testing Agency. Dipa Karmakar's dope sample collected out-of-competition by the ITA, which is an independent organization that manages the antidoping program of the International Gymnastics Federation (FIG) was found to contain Higenamine which is a prohibited substance under World Antidoping Agency Code.

- Kerala has crowned to their bulging cabinet of national football trophies, putting on a show in the final of the National Beach Soccer Championships and overwhelming Punjab 13-4, to win the title, at Dumas Beach, Surat. In the third place game played earlier in the day, Delhi beat Uttarakhand 3-1.

- The central ice hockey team of the Indo-Tibetan Border Police (ITBP) has won the 12th edition of the Ice Hockey Association of India (IHAI) National Ice

Hockey Championship for men- 2023 organized in Leh, Ladakh. The ITBP team defeated the Ladakh Scouts by a score of 1-0 at the final. This is the third time in succession that the mountain trained Force has won this premier national ice hockey championship.

- Australia's longest-serving captain in the shortest format of the game, veteran batter Aaron Finch called time on his international career. Finch, who retired as the One Day International (ODI) captain of the Australian team last year, has confirmed his retirement from T20Is. Finch guided Australia to its maiden ICC World T20 title in 2021.

- France defender Raphael Varane is retiring from international football, ending a 10-year career with Les Bleus in which he won the World Cup in 2018 and was a runner-up four years later. The 29-year-old, who has 93 caps after making his debut in 2013, also helped Didier Deschamps's side win the UEFA Nations League in the 2020-21 season.

- Veteran Pakistan wicketkeeper Kamran Akmal has announced his retirement from all forms of cricket. Prior to the 2023 edition of the Pakistan Super League (PSL). Akmal was earlier named as the batting consultant for the Peshawar Zalmi, led by Babar Azam, for the upcoming edition of the PSL. The 41-year-old said that he is keener on taking up managerial roles with the Pakistan Cricket Board (PCB).

- Gary Ballance, who represented England 42 times across all three formats, scored a superb century for Zimbabwe on the fourth day of the first Test against West Indies in Bulawayo. The 33-year-old's outstanding 137 means he is just the second player in the history of the game to have scored Test centuries for two different countries, following in the footsteps of former Australia and South Africa international Kepler Wessels.

- Indian Olympian Aditi Ashok won the 2023 Magical Kenya Ladies Open Title with a final-round score of 74. This is the fourth Ladies' European championship of Aditi Ashok overall.

- Cristiano Ronaldo scored all of Al Nassr's goals in a 4-0 rout of Al Wehda in the Saudi league as he passed the 500 league goal mark in his club career. The 38-year-old Portuguese star now has 503 goals scored for five different teams stretched across five leagues. The Portuguese superstar scored 103 goals for Manchester United, 311 for Real Madrid, 81 for Juventus, three for Sporting Lisbon. Now, he has five for Al Nassr as well.

- Ravichandran Ashwin picked up his 450th Test wicket during the first Border-Gavaskar Trophy game between India and Australia at the Vidarbha Cricket Association Stadium in Nagpur. He achieved the feat when he bowled Alex Carey in the 54th over. He also became the fastest Indian to scale the landmark, going past former leg-spinner Anil Kumble. Ashwin took 89 Tests to reach the milestone as compared to Kumble's 93.

- Rohit Sharma led from the front as he scored his ninth Test century to become the first Indian captain to score hundreds in all formats. This was Rohit's first three-digit score in the longest format of the game against Australia in the 1st Test of the four-match series for the BorderGavaskar Trophy at the Vidarbha Cricket Association Stadium, Jamtha in Nagpur.

- Real Madrid has won the Club World Cup for a recordextending fifth time after beating Saudi Arabia's AlHilal 5-3 in the final in Rabat, Morocco. Vinícius Júnior scored twice and assisted Karim Benzema to lead Real Madrid to its record-extending eighth Club World Cup title by beating Saudi Arabia's Al-Hilal 5-3.

- Indian batter Smriti Mandhana was the most expensive buy at the inaugural Women's Premier League auction in Mumbai. Royal Challengers Bangalore (RCB) snapped her up for INR 3.4 crore deal. After bagging a whopping amount paid by the RCB in the WPL auction, Mandhana is set to earn double the Pakistan Super League (PSL) highest-paid players.

- Hyundai Motor India Ltd has signed on two more women cricketers named Yastika Bhatia and Renuka Singh Thakur, to its roster of brand ambassadors. Bhatia and Thakur will join Smriti Mandhana, Shafali Verma and Jemimah Rodrigues. The company recognises these women as rising sport stars and that they will be a catalyst in this women's cricket calendar of 2023.

- The U.S. men's national team, along with Mexico and Canada, will automatically qualify for the 2026 FIFA World Cup. The three countries won the right to host the World Cup in a united North American bid. FIFA historically has given host nations the right to play in the World Cup without going through the usual qualification tournaments, though this is the first time FIFA had to set aside three host bids.

- Sania Mirza has been roped in as mentor of Royal Challengers Bangalore for the inaugural Women's Premier League (WPL), to be played in Mumbai from March 4 to 26. The franchise also announced the signing of Australian Ben Sawyer as head coach. Sawyer is the head coach of New Zealand Women and was part of the Women's World Cup-winning side with Australia last year as the assistant coach.

- Virat Kohli became the sixth and the fastest batter in the world to score 25,000 runs across formats during the second Test against Australia, which India won by six wickets. He had come into his 492nd match overall with 52 runs needed to reach the milestone. He scored 44 runs in India's first innings before being dismissed for 20 runs to finish with 25012 runs.

- England Test captain Ben Stokes became the player to hit the most number of sixes in the history of Test cricket, surpassing England coach and former New Zealand cricketer Brendon McCullum in the match against New Zealand. In 90 Test matches, Stokes scored a total of 5,652 runsat an average of 36.00 with 109 sixes and 12 centuries and 28 fifties. His individual best score in Tests is 258.

- Saurashtra defeated Bengal by nine wickets to clinch its second Ranji Trophy 2022-23 title at the Eden Gardens in Kolkata. Saurashtra won their second Ranji Trophy title at the Eden Gardens in Kolkata. Saurashtra won the Ranji Trophy title for the first time in 2019-20.

- The Board of Control for Cricket in India (BCCI) is close to agreeing to a deal with German sporting goods giant Adidas to pay Rs 350 crore as the team's uniform sponsor.

- After winning the 24th NordWest Cup 2023 at Bad Zwischenahn in Germany and defeating German IM Ilja Schneider, Indian chess player Vignesh NR became the 80th Grandmaster of India.

- Indian teen Tilottama Sen won the bronze medal in the women's 10m Air Rifle at ISSF World Cup 2023 in Cairo in Egypt. The 14-year-old Tilottama Sen won the second bronze for India, fifth overall after ending the top eight ranking round with a score of 262. She missed out on the gold medal match by a narrow possible margin of 0.1. Great Britain's Seonaid Mcintosh won gold and Switzerland's Olympic Champion Nina Christen came second to win silver.

- Top-seeded Spanish player, Carlos Alcaraz won his first title since his milestone U.S. Open triumph by beating Cameron Norrie in straight sets at the Argentina Open tennis Tournament.

- Paris Saint-Germain's and former Real Madrid defender Sergio Ramos has announced that he is retiring from international football. After a record 180 appearances for Spain. Ramos, who was part of Spain's World Cup and Euro winning teams had represented Real Madrid in La Liga and now plays for PSG in Ligue 1.

- India's Rudrankksh Balasaheb Patil won the men's 10m air rifle event at the ISSF World Cup 2023 in Cairo. He defeated Germany's Maximilian Ullbrich by 16-8 in the gold medal match to clinch the top prize. Rudrankksh Patil finished seventh in the qualification round with 629.3 points to make the ranking round, which he topped with 262.0 points to set up a final clash against Ulbrich.

- Daniil Medvedev won the Qatar Open in his professional tennis debut by defeating Andy Murray 64, 6-4, in the final game between two former No. 1s. In every set, Medvedev converted quick beginnings. In the first, he got to 4-1, and in the second, he got to 3-1.

- Hockey Madhya Pradesh was named the winner of the 13th Hockey India Senior Women National Championship in 2023 after defeating Hockey Maharashtra 5-1 in the championship game in Kakinada, Andhra Pradesh. In the meantime, Hockey Jharkhand finished third after winning the third-place game against Hockey Haryana.

- The all-time great Lionel Messi has scored his 700th career club goal in Paris St. Germain's 3-0 win over Marseille. With the goal, Messi became just the second player in history to score 700 career club goals, according to IFFHS (International Federation of Football History and Statistics).

- Argentina's Lionel Messi has bagged the Best FIFA men's player prize for 2022. Messi outclassed his Paris Saint Germain (PSG) teammate Kylian Mbappe and Real Madrid captain Karim Benzema to lift the famous trophy at Salle Pleyel in Paris.

Summits And Conferences

- The 30th National Child Science Congress was inaugurated on 27th January 2023 at Ahmedabad, Gujarat. The National Child Science Congress is a fiveday event that was held at Science City. The event was concluded on 31st January 2023. The National Child Science Congress was organized by the Gujarat Council on Science and Technology (GUJCOST), the Gujarat Council of Science City, and SAL Education.

- The Secretary of the Ministry of Electronics and Information Technology (MeitY), Alkesh Kumar Sharma inaugurated the G20 Cyber Security Exercise and Drill for more than 400 domestic and international participants under India's G20 presidency.

- The first Youth20 (Y20) Inception Meeting 2023 under G20 began in Guwahati. Briefing the media ahead of the meeting Meeta Rajivlochan, Secretary, Ministry of Youth Affairs informed that Youth20 deliberations hope to reach out to youth and consult with them for their ideas for a better future.

- Prime Minister Narendra Modi inaugurated the Uttar Pradesh Global Investors Summit 2023 in Lucknow. The 10-12 February event is expected to be attended by several ministers of the Union and the state government and a host of leading industrialists.

- The World Government Summit 2023 is set to begin on 13th February 2023 in Dubai. The World Government Summit will be held under the theme of "Shaping Future Governments". It will bring together global thought leaders, global experts, and decision-makers to share and contribute to the development of tools, policies, and models that will be critical in shaping future governments.

- Peter Burwash International (PBI), one of the top tennis instruction programmes, has partnered with the Ileseum Club in Bavdhan, Pune, to open a second training facility there. Rene Zondag, president of PBI, announced the opening of the new centre, which spans 12.5 acres and offers top-notch amenities.

- The 2nd Indian Rice Congress 2023 was inaugurated in Cuttack by President Droupadi Murmu in the presence of Odisha Governor Prof. Ganeshi Lal, Union Minister of Agriculture and Farmers Welfare, Narendra Singh Tomar, and Odisha Minister of Agriculture and Farmers Empowerment, Fisheries, and Animal Resource Development, Ranendra Pratap Swain.

- DHARA, Driving Holistic Action for Urban Rivers, the annual meeting of the members of the River Cities Alliance (RCA) is organized by the National Mission for Clean Ganga (NMGC), partnered with the National Institute of Urban Affairs (NIUA) from 13th to 14th February 2023 in Pune.

- External Affairs Minister S Jaishankar and Fiji Prime Minister Sitiveni Rabuka to inaugurate the three-day event' the 12th World Hindi Conference on 15th February at the Pacific Island nation. The 12th World Hindi Conference, scheduled to be held at Nadi from 15th February to 17th February 2023, will be on the theme "Hindi - Traditional Knowledge to Artificial Intelligence".

- The Minister for Communications, Electronics & Information Technology and Railways, Ashwini Vaishnaw inaugurated the 'SemiconIndia Conference of Electronics Manufacturing Supply Chain Ecosystem'. The government is 'willing to walk the talk' and Its "Say-do" ratio is very high with readiness to receive feedback and sustain industry efforts for a lperiodtime.

- A 3-day long 18th UIC World Security Congress jointly organised by the International Union of Railways (UIC), Paris and the Railway Protection Force (RPF) began on 21 February. Theme of this year's Congress is "Railway Security Strategy: Responses and Vision for Future".

- A vice-ministerial level meeting of I2U2 countries including Israel, India, the United States, and the United Arab Emirates discussed with private sector stakeholders investment opportunities to address issues related to the management of the energy crisis and food insecurity. The UAE hosted the first vice-ministerial meeting of the I2U2 in Abu Dhabi which was attended by senior officials from the four countries, along with representations from the private sector.

- The Ajanta Ellora International Festival 2023 was held from 25th February to 27th February in Aurangabad, Maharashtra. The Ajanta Ellora International Festival 2023 festival is a celebration of the cultural heritage and diversity of the region and promises to be a feast for the senses. The festival showcases the Ellora and Ajanta caves' artwork and architecture, as well as performances by local and international artists.

- The Youth 20 India Summit will be held at the Maharaja Sayajirao University Vadodara in Gujarat which was attended by more than 600 delegates from 62 countries. The international conference of The Youth 20 India Summit was inaugurated by Bhupendra Patel, Chief Minister of Gujarat.

- The 19th annual Commonwealth Parliamentary Association (CPA), India Zone-3 conference, inaugurated by Lok Sabha Speaker Om Birla, on February 23 at Gangtok, Sikkim.

- The World Book Fair began in New Delhi where books from all genres from children to students to adults are showcased for everyone. In the World Book Fair, there is the participation of over 30 countries and nearly 1,000 publishers and exhibitors, the New Delhi World Book Fair (NDWBF) is returning to its full physical form after a gap of three years.

Awards & Recognition

- Former prime minister Dr Manmohan Singh was recently conferred a Lifetime Achievement Honour by the India-UK Achievers Honours in London for his contribution to economic and political life.

- In the Finals of FIH Odisha Hockey Men's World Cup 2023 Bhubaneswar-Rourkela, FIH President Tayyab Ikram presented the FIH President's Award to VK Pandian, Secretary to the Chief Minister of Odisha, for his commendable contribution to hockey. The FIH President highlighted the crucial role played by CM Naveen Patnaik along with VK Pandian in hosting a glorious Hockey World Cup.

- Five athletes were nominated for the BBC Indian Sportswoman of the Year award, including wrestlers Vinesh Phogat and Sakshi Malik, who recently protested WFI president Brij Bhushan Sharan Singh and accused him of sexual abuse and intimidation.

- Managing Director & CEO, Manappuram Finance Ltd, VP Nandakumar has bagged the Hurun India's award for his remarkable achievements in the world of business. V.K. Mathews, founder and executive chairman, IBS Software, has been conferred the Hurun Industry Achievement Award 2022.

- MRF Ltd. Chairman and Managing Director K.M. Mammen was presented the ATMA Lifetime Achievement Award by Maruti Suzuki India MD & CEO Hisashi Takeuchi at the Automotive Tyre Manufacturers' Association (ATMA) Annual Conclave 2023 in New Delhi.

- The country's largest power generating company, NTPC Limited has been honoured with 'ATD Best Awards 2023' by the Association for Talent Development (ATD), USA. This is the sixth time that NTPC Limited has won this award for demonstrating enterprise success in the field of talent development. The foundation of NTPC's culture has always been to engage employees through creative techniques. The award is testimony to NTPC's contemporary HR practices.

- In 2023, the Raja Ram Mohan Roy National Award is presented to Journalist A.B.K. Prasad for his contributions towards journalism. Raja Ram Mohan Roy lived in the 19th century. The reformer founded Brahmo Samaj in 1828 and played a major role in abolishing Sati. The Press Council of India presents awards in the name of the legend every year. - For her assistance to refugees in Germany, former German chancellor Angela Merkel was awarded the UNESCO peace prize. According to Politico, the former German leader received the UN prize for her choice to accept the refugees into German territory back in 2015.

- Writer Subhash Chandran's novel Samudrashila has been chosen for the Akbar Kakkattil Award instituted by a trust in the memory of the short story writer and novelist from Kozhikode. The novel was selected by a three-member jury from among the literary works published in the last five years.

- The 'Don't Choose Extinction' campaign, launched by the UN Development Programme (UNDP) to raise awareness about the climate emergency, has won Gold and Silver in two different categories at the 2nd Annual Anthem Awards. This was announced by the International Academy of Digital Arts & Science (IADAS), which was launched by the Webby Awards in 2021. The Awards are intended to celebrate mission-driven work and the social impact of individuals, corporations and organizations. Its goal is to define a new benchmark for impactful work that inspires others to take action in their communities.

- The Kollam district panchayat has won the Swaraj Trophy for the best district panchayat in the State for the 2021-22 financial year. The Kannur district panchayat stood second in the rankings.

- A software engineer of Indian descent who later became a hobbyist photographer has been named the grand prize winner of National Geographic's "Pictures of the Year" competition. In the year 2020, Karthik Subramaniam began experimenting with his camera after being quarantined at his San Francisco, California, house as a result of the epidemic.

- Poet V. Madhusoodanan Nair has been selected for the Jnanappana Award - 2023 instituted by the Guruvayur Devaswom. The award carries ₹50,001, a gold locket of Guruvayurappan and a citation. It will be presented to the poet by Minister for Higher Education R. Bindu at a cultural meet to be held at Melpathur Auditorium, Guruvayur.

- Dr. Mahendra Kumar Mishra, an Indian educator and social worker for the advancement of indigenous languages in Odisha, received the World Mother Language Award from Prime Minister Sheikh Hasina in Dhaka, Bangladesh.

- Sajjan Jindal, the chairman and managing director of JSW Group, was awarded as the EY Entrepreneur of the Year (EOY) 2022.

- SS Rajamouli's directorial, 'RRR' has bagged the 'Best International Film' award at the Hollywood Critics Association Film Awards. The film director Rajamouli and actor Ram Charan accepted the award with joy and pride. It has also won three more awards at the HCA film awards. Before bagging the 'Best International Film' award, 'RRR' won three awards at HCA - 'Best Action Film', 'Best Stunts', and 'Best Original Song'.

- Computer scientist Hari Balakrishnan has been awarded the 2023 Marconi Prize. Dr. Balakrishnan has been cited "for fundamental contributions to wired and wireless networking, mobile sensing, and distributed systems". The Marconi Prize is a top honour for computer scientists and is awarded by the U.S.-based Marconi Foundation.

- The India Today Tourism Survey has chosen Jammu & Kashmir Tourism for best adventure tourism award. The awards were given away at New Delhi by Union Minister of State for Culture & Parliamentary Affairs, Arjun Ram Meghwal.

Important Days

- World Interfaith Harmony Week is an annual event observed during the first week of February (1-7), after General Assembly designation in 2010. These celebrations focus on creating mutual understanding and interreligious dialogue to promote harmony between people regardless of their faith.

- World Wetlands Day is celebrated annually on 2nd February. The day is observed to create awareness among people about the importance of wetlands and different ways to restore their rapid loss and degradation. The day is aimed at highlighting the vital role wetlands play in maintaining biodiversity and supporting human well-being. The theme for this year's World Wetlands Day is 'It's Time for Wetlands Restoration. The theme highlights the urgency to prioritize wetland restoration.

- The International Day of Human Fraternity was established by the United Nations General Assembly on December 21, 2020. The International Day of Human Fraternity has been observed every year on February 4. This day, which falls in the middle of the International Interfaith Harmony Week is recognised by one of the world's leading transnational organisations- the United Nations. - Each year on February 4, World Cancer Day is celebrated worldwide. It is believed to have brought everyone together in the fight against cancer. World Cancer Day seeks to save millions of lives by educating the public, promoting awareness, and pressuring individuals and governments around the world to take action every year.

- International Day of Zero Tolerance for Female Genital Mutilation (FGM) is observed on February 6. This year, the UNFPA-UNICEF Joint Programme on the Elimination of Female Genital Mutilation: Delivering the Global Promise launched the 2023 theme; "Partnership with Men and Boys to transform Social and gender Norms to End FGM".

- This year's Safer Internet Day took place on Tuesday, 7 February 2023. Significantly, it was the 20th edition of the campaign. Safer Internet Day is marked to help the younger generation understand safe practices on the Internet. According to UK Safer Internet Center, the theme for Safer Internet Day 2023 is 'Want to talk about it? Making space for conversations about life online.' This year, the day will be commemorated on February 7.

- Every year World Pulses Day is celebrated on February 10 with an aim to spread awareness about the nutritional and environmental benefits of pulses as part of sustainable food production. 'Pulses for a Sustainable Future' as the theme for the 2023 celebration.

- The United Nations General Assembly has designated February 11 as the International Day of Women and Girls in Science to recognise the significant contribution that women make to the fields of science and technology. The theme for the 8th International Day of Women and Girls in Science is "Innovate. Demonstrate. Elevate. Advance (IDEA): Bringing communities Forward for sustainable and equitable development."

- The National Deworming Day is observed on February 10 every year. It is an initiative taken by the Government of India to deworm all the children across the nation in the age group of 1 to 19.

- World Radio Day is celebrated every year on February 13 to mark the important role that radio plays in our lives and in society. In 2023, the theme for the World Radio Day is "Radio and Peace" which aims to focus on the importance of independent radio to foster peace and prevent conflict.

- World Unani Day is observed on February 11 every year to commemorate the birth anniversary of social reformer and renowned Unani scholar Hakim Ajmal Khan, widely regarded as the pioneer of Unani medicine in India. The Central Council for Research in Unani Medicine, Ministry of AYUSH, host an international conference on Unani medicine in a hybrid virtual mode with the theme "Unani Medicine for Public Health" in Delhi.

- The annual celebration of National Productivity Day is observed on February 12, coordinated by the National Productivity Council (NPC). The NPC's mission is to promote awareness towards increasing the productivity of the country. The day is celebrated as part of National Productivity Week, which is observed from February 12 to 18. This year's National Productivity Day theme is "Productivity, Green Growth, and Sustainability: Celebrating India's G20 Presidency."

- Every year on February 13, the nation commemorates Sarojini Naidu's birth anniversary. The 144th anniversary of Sarojini Naidu's birth is this year. She was well-known in India as a poet, politician, and administrator.

- International Childhood Cancer Day (ICCD) is observed on February 15 every year. The day was observed by the Childhood Cancer International, an umbrella organisation of various child cancer support groups created by parents. The three-year campaign for International Childhood Cancer Day began in 2021 and will conclude in 2023. The theme for the three-year campaign is 'Better Survival'.

- The United Nations General Assembly has adopted a resolution from Jamaica to declare the first-ever Global Tourism Resilience Day on 17th February 2023, in an effort to future-proof the sustainability of tourism.

- World Pangolin Day is observed annually on the third Saturday in February, and this year it falls on February 18. It is a day to remember and celebrate pangolins, raise awareness, and fight against global pangolin capture in Africa and Asia.

- India celebrates Soil Health Card Day on February 19 every year to remember the beginning of the Soil Health Card (SHC) Scheme and to raise awareness of its advantages.

- World Day of Social Justice is observed annually on February 20. The main goal of this day is to raise a voice against social injustice and to bring together diverse communities around the world in an effort to eradicate poverty, physical discrimination, gender inequalities, religious discrimination and illiteracy, and create a society that is socially integrated. This year's theme focuses on the recommendations of Our Common Agenda to strengthen global solidarity and to re-build trust in government by "Overcoming Barriers and Unleashing Opportunities for Social Justice".

- Every year on February 21, the world celebrates International Mother Language Day to encourage linguistic, cultural, and multilingualism variety. The theme of the 2023 International Mother Language Day, "Multilingual education - a necessity to transform education".

- Every year on February 22, the World Organization of Girl Guides and Girl Scouts (WAGGGS) observes World Thinking Day. 'Our World, Our Peaceful Future', the theme for World Thinking Day 2023, explores what one can understand from the ecosystem and how we can cooperate with nature to build a more secure and tranquil future for girls worldwide.

- World Scout Day is observed annually on February 22 by millions of Boy Scouts worldwide. It honours Lord Robert Baden-Powell, who founded the Boy Scout Movement, on the day of his birthday. The day is observed by National Scout Organizations all over the world through events including fundraising campaigns, food drives, and other types of volunteer work.

- Every year on February 24, Central Excise Day is observed to recognise and honour the contributions made by the Central Board of Indirect Taxes and Customs (CBIC).

- The World NGO Day is an annual international observance on February **27** to recognize the contributions of non-governmental organizations (NGOs).

- On February 28 each year, National Science Day honours Chandrasekhara Venkata Raman as C.V. Raman, an Indian scientist and physician, for discovering the "Raman Effect." Every year, it is celebrated to honour the value of science and to serve as a reminder of the influence it has had on humankind's way of life. In honour of India's G20 leadership, the event this year has the theme "Global Science for Global Wellness."

Defence Current Affairs

- The Indian Coast Guard (ICG) is celebrating its 47th Raising Day on 1st February 2023. From a modest beginning with just seven surface platforms in 1978, the ICG today has 158 ships and 78 aircraft and is likely to achieve the targeted force levels of 200 surface platforms and 80 aircraft by 2025.

- A joint training exercise "Exercise Trishakri Prahar" was conducted in North Bengal from 21 January to 31 January 2023. The aim of the exercise was to practice battle preparedness of the Security Forces using the latest weapons and equipment in a networked, integrated environment, involving all arms and services of the Army, the Indian Air Force and CAPFs. Exercise culminated on 31 January 2023 with an Integrated Fire Power Exercise in Teesta Field Firing Ranges.

- As part of "Operation Dost," India is deploying a field hospital, supplies, and rescue personnel to the earthquake-stricken countries of Turkey and Syria. A 7.8-magnitude earthquake that occurred while people were asleep destroyed thousands of buildings, trapped an undetermined number of people, and may have affected millions of people.

- The Ministry of Defence on February 8 inked a contract with Larsen & Toubro (L&T) for the purchase of 41 indigenous modular bridges for the Corps of Engineers of the Indian Army, valued at over Rs 2,585 crore, providing a significant boost to the "Aatmanirbar Bharat" initiative.

- The Hindustan Aeronautics Limited (HAL) has unveiled the Hindustan Lead-in Fighter Trainer (HLFT-42) design of the scale model at the 14th edition of Aero

India 2023 held in Bengaluru. The HLFT-42 aircraft design includes a unique rail art of the Hindu God Maruti, symbolizing strength, speed, and agility. HAL did a project named HF42 Marut. Marut means spirit of the winds. The aircraft similar configuration.

- NewSpace Research, a Bengaluru-based start-up has delivered SWARM drones to Indian Army, which makes the Army the first major armed force in the world to operationalise these high-density SWARM drones. This delivery may possibly be the world's first operational high density swarming UAS (Unmanned Aerial System) induction for military applications, especially given that most swarm drone research is yet to be operationalised across the world.

- Drone startup Garuda Aerospace has unveiled its solarpowered drone "SURAJ", designed specifically for surveillance operations, at Aero India 2023. SURAJ is an ISR (intelligence, surveillance, reconnaissance) highaltitude drone designed specifically for surveillance operations, providing "real-time information to the high command and protecting jawans on the ground."

- In Aero India, the Hindustan Aeronautics Ltd has received the Indian Technical Standard Order (ITSO) authorisation from Directorate General of Civil Aviation (DGCA) for its indigenously developed Cockpit Voice Recorder (CVR) and Flight Data Recorder (FDR). CVR and FDR are popularly known as 'black boxes'.

- Defence Minister Rajnath Singh launched the 'iDEX Investor Hub' (iIH), under which more than Rs 200 crores had already been pledged by leading Indian investors. Defence Minister also launched the ninth edition of 'Defence India Startup Challenges (DISC 9)' on "Cybersecurity" during the annual defense innovation event 'Manthan' as part of the Aero India 2023.

- A joint counter-terrorism exercise Tarkash between National Security Guard (NSG) and US Special Operations Forces (SOF) culminated in Chennai, after four weeks of intense training and joint anti-terror exercises. The main highlight of the exercise was mock drills for the CBRN (Chemical, Biological, Radiological and Nuclear) counter terror response by special forces of both countries.

- India and Japan has kick started an exercise 'Ex Dharma Guardian' at Camp Imazu in Shiga Province, Japan from February 17 to March 2, 2023. The Indian Army contingent arrived at the exercise location on February 12, 2023.

- The Indian Air Force has developed an innovative solution 'Vayulink' that would aid pilots in dealing with bad weather and also provide jammer-proof uninterrupted communication with the base station. The data link communication uses the Indian Regional Navigation Satellite System (IRNSS) that is also known as NAVIC, to send radio communication to the base station when the signals are low.

- Navratna Defence PSU Bharat Electronics Ltd (BEL) has signed an MoU with Israel Aerospace Industries (IAI) for the domestic manufacture and supply of its LongRange Artillery Weapon System (LORA) for the Indian Tri-services. This state-of-the-art strategic weapon system will be manufactured by BEL, as the prime contractor, based on the workshare arrangement with IAI.

- The fourth iteration of the biennial training exercise DUSTLIK (2023) will be held in Pithoragarh, Uttarakhand, from February 20, 2023 through March 5, 2023, as part of a military-to-military exchange programme between the Indian Army and the Uzbekistan Army.

- In commemoration of India's late Chief of Defence Staff General Bipin Rawat, a bell has been placed at Nepal's revered Shree Muktinath Temple. The bell named "Bipin Bell," has been installed at the revered Hindu temple in Mustang district during the visit of four former Indian army chiefs namely Gen VN Sharma, Gen JJ Singh, Gen Deepak Kapoor and Gen Dalbir Suhag.

- Malabar multilateral naval exercise will be hosted by Australia for the first time this year, which includes participation from India, Australia, Japan, and the United States.

- India and Seychelles signed six agreements in key areas, including maritime security, and on sharing of white shipping information that would enable the two countries to exchange data regarding identity and movement of non-military commercial vessels.

- The Chief of the Naval Staff Adm R Harikumar visited INS Nireekshak at Kochi where he interacted with the diving team of the ship involved in the salvage operations at a depth of 219 meters in the Arabian Sea. He commended the ship on the safe and successful conduct of the operations under the most challenging circumstances. This is the deepest salvage carried out in the country's waters.

- The Central Reserve Police Force (CRPF) will hold its Raising Day function in the Bastar district of Chhattisgarh for the first time, a place that has been a hotbed of left-wing extremism. The preparation for the celebration on March 19 will start in a few days.

- In line with the expanding military cooperation with South East Asian nations, an Indian Navy Kilo class conventional submarine, INS Sindhukesari, docked in Jakarta, Indonesia, for the first time. The submarine, which was on operational deployment, travelled through the Sunda Strait and undertook the maiden docking in Indonesia for Operational Turnaround (OTR). Naval ships regularly make port calls to countries in the region.

- The Tawazun Council signed 11 deals, worth Dhs5.8bn ($1.579bn), on the third day of the International Defence Exhibition (IDEX) and the Naval Defence Exhibition (NAVDEX) 2023. A total of nine deals were inked with local and international companies on behalf of the Ministry of Defence, and two contracts worth Dhs 134 m were sealed on behalf of Abu Dhabi Police.

- For the first time, India's indigenously made light combat aircraft Tejas will be participating in an international multilateral air exercise - Exercise Desert Flag VIll - in the UAE, reflecting India's increasing efforts at showcasing the jet at the world stage.

Science and Technology

- ISRO and Indian Institute of Technology Madras (IIT Madras) plans to develop a training module for the Indian Spaceflight Programme using Augmented Reality / Virtual Reality / Mixed Reality (AR / VR / MR). ISRO aims to utilise the advanced technologies created at the newly established eXperiential Technology

Innovation Centre (XTIC) at IIT Madras to promote Research and Development (R&D) in the domain of Extended Reality.

- Google has unveiled an experimental conversation AI service called "Bard", as it races to catch up with the wildly popular chatbot ChatGPT from the Microsoft-backed firm OpenAI. According to Alphabet CEO Sundar Pichai, the service will be initially opened up to "trusted testers" before making it more widely available to the public in the coming weeks.

- NASA's "all-electric" plane X – 57 is soon set to take off, the US space agency. The plane has 14 propellers along its wings and is powered entirely by electricity. Recently, NASA's X-57 Maxwell performed successful thermal testing of its cruise motor controllers. Thermal testing is important because it validates the design, operability, and workmanship quality of aircraft controllers. The controllers have temperature-sensitive parts and must be able to withstand extreme conditions during flight.

- The battle for the most known moons in the Solar System is raging on. After losing its lead to Saturn in 2019, Jupiter has once again surged ahead. Astronomers have counted 12 previously unknown moons in orbit around our Solar System's biggest planet, bringing the known total to 92, and leaving Saturn, with its measly count of 83, in the dust.

- Chinese search engine Baidu revealed its plans of launching a ChatGPT-style AI chatbot called 'Ernie Bot'. Baidu's Hong Kong-listed shares jumped as much as 13.4% on the news. Ernie, meaning "Enhanced Representation through Knowledge Integration," is a large AI-powered language model introduced in 2019.

- SpaceX intends to fire up all 33 of its engines before launching its massive Starship launch system into orbit for the first time. This is an important step in the company's mission to the moon and Mars. Gwynne Shotwell, president and chief operating officer, announced at an industry conference that the so-called static fire is slated.

- Union Minister for Road Transport and Highways Nitin Gadkari unveiled Skye UTM, which is the most cuttingedge unmanned traffic management system in the world, which is capable of handling 4,000 flights per hour and 96,000 flights per day. Skye UTM is a Cloud-based aerial traffic management system that integrates unmanned air traffic with manned aviation airspace.

- National Aeronautics and Space Administration (NASA) and the Indian Space Research Organisation (ISRO), jointly developed an Earth-observation satellite, called NISAR (NASA-ISR0 Synthetic Aperture Radar), got a send-off ceremony at the American space agency's Jet Propulsion Laboratory (JPL) in Southern California.

- The Indian Space Research Organisation (ISR0) successfully launched the second edition of the Small Satellite Launch Vehicle (SSLV-D2) from the first launch pad of Satish Dhawan space centre at Sriharikota, Andhra Pradesh.

- Jeff Bezos-led Blue Origin scored a big contract from the American space agency, Nasa, to launch a mission to Mars. The private space company was given its first interplanetary NASA contract to launch the mission to study the magnetic field around the Red Planet. The expected launch date for the mission is 2024.

- Alphabet Inc. lost $100 billion in market value shortly after its new chatbot inadvertently disclosed false information in a promotional video. While Microsoft shares jumped almost 3% before losing some of their gains, its shares fell as much as 9% during regular trade. Initially, Reuters called attention to a mistake in Google's advertisement for its debuting chatbot Bard.

- The Science Center and Planetarium will be constructed in Kota, Rajasthan. The Science Center and Planetarium will be one of the best science centers and planetariums in the world. About 35 crore 25 lakh rupees will be spent on these. An MoU was signed between the National Council of Science Museums and the Science and Technology Department of the Government of Rajasthan in this regard.

- Antaris announced that the world's first satellite fully conceived, designed, and manufactured using the company's end-to-end cloud platform, JANUS-1 has successfully reached orbit. JANUS-1 rode on the Indian Space Research Organization's (ISRO) SSLV-D2 rocket Intel has launched the new Xeon W-3400 and Xeon

W2400 desktop workstation processors (code-named Sapphire Rapids), which are built for professional creators to provide massive performance for media and entertainment, engineering, and data science professionals. According to Intel, the new workstation processors are available for pre-order from industry partners, with system availability beginning in March.

- Intel has launched the new Xeon W-3400 and Xeon W2400 desktop workstation processors (code-named Sapphire Rapids), which are built for professional creators to provide massive performance for media and entertainment, engineering, and data science professionals. According to Intel, the new workstation processors are available for pre-order from industry partners, with system availability beginning in March.

- Lexi, a ChatGPT-powered AI chatbot, has arrived in India. Velocity, a financial technology firm, launched the chatbot to assist e-commerce owners by presenting them with business information in a simplified manner. Velocity insights, Velocity's proprietary analytics platform, has been linked with the chatbot.

- Anil Agarwal-led Vedanta and manufacturing behemoth Foxconn announced their joint venture's plans to build a semiconductor and display manufacturing facility in Gujarat's Dholera Special Investment Zone.

- Serum Institute of India will be setting up Dr. Cyrus Poonawalla Centre of Excellence (CoE) in Infectious Diseases and Pandemic Preparedness in the Indian Institute of Public Health, Hyderabad.

- The Martin Foundation in association with Dr APJ Abdul Kalam International Foundation and Space Zone India launched the APJ Abdul Kalam Satellite Launch Vehicle Mission-2023 from the Pattipolam village of Chengalpattu district in Tamil Nadu. Telangana Governor Tamilisai Soundararajan was also present at the event.

- At ELECRAMA 2023, the largest solo electrical exhibition in the world held at the India Expo Mart in Greater Noida, the Ministry of Power, Government of India displayed a number of advances in the energy sector.

- Minister for IT and Industries KT Rama Rao informed that the World Health Organisation will set up an mRNA (messenger ribonucleic acid) vaccine hub in Telangana. mRNA is becoming a promising technology to address a growing number of infectious diseases.

- India's first hybrid sounding rocket by private players was successfully launched from Pattipulam village in the Chengalpattu district of Tamil Nadu. Martin Foundation, in association with Dr. APJ Abdul Kalam International Foundation and Space Zone India, launched the Dr. APJ Abdul Kalam Satellite Launch Vehicle Mission- 2023.

- India's largest IT services company Tata Consultancy Services (TCS) announced that it has won a deal to digitally transform Telefonica Germany's specific operations. The latter is a leading German telecom company. The Indian IT services exporter announced that the partnership would entail building service assurance applications and processes within the Operations Support Systems (OSS) landscape of the German telecom company.

- Artifact, a new artificial intelligence (AI)-powered personalized news feed application by Instagram cofounders Kevin Systrom and Mike Krieger, is available to everyone, along with new features. Now, anyone can download and use the new application and no waitlist or phone number is required. The application is available for both iOS and Android users.

- Facebook co-founder Mark Zuckerberg announced Meta Platforms' impending release to researchers of a new large language model called LLaMA (Large Language Model Meta AI).

Books & Authors

- A two-volume box set, 'The Best of Satyajit Ray' published by Penguin Random House India, is not only a treat for Ray enthusiasts but also a collector's edition. A new anthology offers a glimpse into the fiction and non-fiction writings of the legendary filmmaker and polymath Satyajit Ray. The book set picks from the everpopular adventures of Ray's enduring creation, the professional sleuth,

Feluda, to the chronicles of Professor Shonku, his short stories as well as writings on filmmaking, and his thoughts on world and Indian cinema.

- Salman Rushdie published his new novel "Victory City", an "epic tale" of a 14th-century woman who defies a patriarchal world to rule a city. The much-anticipated work tells the tale of young orphan girl Pampa Kampana who is endowed by a goddess with magical powers and founds the city, in modern-day India, of Bisnaga, which translates as Victory City.

- BJP national president J.P. Nadda has launched a book "Modi: Shaping a Global Order in Flux" in Chanakyapuri. Book is forewarded by Union External Affair Minister S. Jaishankar. Editors are Sujan Chinoy, Vijay Chauthaiwala, and Uttam Kumar Sinha. This book is going to open a debate on how PM Modi has taken a decision which has changed India's image worldwide. It's necessary to understand what was the image of India before Modi ji came to power. The publisher of the book is Wisdom Tree.

Miscellaneous Current Affairs

- An international sand artist named Sudarsan Pattnaik made a sand sculpture of the late singer Lata Mangeshkar at Puri Beach in the state of Odisha to commemorate her first death anniversary. With the words "Tribute to Bharat Ratna Lata Ji, Meri Awaaz Hi Pehechan Hai," he built a stunning sculpture. Using around 5 tonnes of sand and a 6-foot-tall sand sculpture of the late singer that included a massive gramophone record, Pattnaik built it.

- Yaya Tso, known as birds' paradise for its beautiful lake located at an altitude of 4,820 metres, has been proposed as Ladakh's first biodiversity heritage site (BHS). The Biodiversity Management Committee, the panchayat of Chumathang village, along with SECURE Himalaya Project recently resolved to declare Yaya Tso as Ladakh's first BHS under the Biological Diversity Act.

- Indore Municipal Corporation has ranked top in cleanliness survey for six consecutive years, has become the country's first civic body to launch green bonds, seeking to raise Rs 244 crore for a 60-mw solar plant at its water pumping station. The public issues of the green bonds will be open for subscription from February 10-14. The issue will be listed on the National Stock Exchange.

- The Indian government issued urgent and emergency orders to restrict 138 betting and gambling applications and 94 loan-providing apps. Players including PayU's LazyPay, Kissht, and numerous more loan apps were impacted by the prohibition.

- The Sculpture Park at Bikaner House in New Delhi was inaugurated by Rajasthan Chief Secretary Usha Sharma. Sculpture Park showcases a fusion of modern and contemporary art and culture in the traditional setting of Bikaner House. The Sculpture Park is a trailblazer in the national capital and offers a premier platform for emerging artists to showcase their work with ease.

- Visva-Bharati University was founded by Rabindranath in 1921. It will soon receive the UNESCO 'heritage" tag. This will allow it to be the first university of living heritage. Bidyut Chakraborty, Vice-Chancellor of Visva-Bharati University, stated that the university would be designated a heritage university.

- Glass igloo restaurant has been opened in the middle of the snow-covered mountains in Gulmarg and has become the center of attraction for tourists in the hill station in Kashmir. Tourists are seen enjoying their meals and taking photographs in the glass-wall restaurant. This unique glass igloo restaurant is developed by Kolahoi Green Heights, a hotel in Gulmarg.

- Google honored PK Rosy who became the first female lead in Malayalam cinema with a doodle. PK Rosy was born on 10th February 1903 in Thiruvananthapuram formerly known as Trivandrum. Google remembers PK Rosy, the first woman leader in Malayalam on her 120th birth anniversary. She was the first actress to work in Malayalam films with JC Daniel's Vigathakumaran.

- Ministry of Tribal Affairs in Lok Sabha has revealed that the National Commission for Scheduled Tribes (NCST) is currently functioning with less than 50% of its sanctioned strength. According to data from the Commission, rules provide for the ST panel to have one Chairperson, one Vice-Chairperson, and three Members (two among V-C and Members must be from ST community). Currently, it just has a Chairperson (Harsh Chouhan) and one Member (Ananta Nayak) with all other positions, including that of the mandatory ST Member, vacant for the last three years.

- GA Infra Pvt Ltd, a leading infrastructure company in India, has been awarded the contract for designing and constructing the country's first National Metro Rail Knowledge Centre. The centre will be located at the Vishwavidyalaya Metro Station in Delhi and built on a Public-Private Partnership (PPP) model.

- The Government of India has launched a mobile app "KhananPrahari" and a web app Coal Mine Surveillance and Management System (CMSMS) for reporting unauthorized coal mining activities so that monitoring and taking suitable action on it can be done by the concerned Law & Order enforcing authority.

- The Pangong Tso Lake in Ladakh will host the first-ever frozen lake marathon on 20th February 2023, at an altitude of roughly 13,862 feet. The first-ever frozen lake marathon which is of 21-kilometer is India's first of its kind. The marathon will occur at a height of 13,862 feet and it will be the first of its kind to ever take place in the globe at this altitude.

- A new beetle species have been discovered in India, according to a paper published in the New Zealandbased journal Zootaxa. The beetle is important for forensic science as it helps detect the time of death of an animal or human. Omorgus Khandesh is necrophagous and is also called a keratin beetle.

- Worldwide, populations of domestic poultry and wild birds are being decimated by The Largest Reported outbreak of avian influenza. There are growing concerns that it could be harmful to people as well. The World Health Organization's Tedros Adhanom Ghebreyesus issued a warning on February 8 urging everyone to get ready for a potential bird flu pandemic.

- Divya Kala Mela 2023 is a unique event showcasing the products and craftsmanship of Divyang entrepreneurs/artisans from across the country and has been started in Mumbai. The Divya Kala Mela 2023 is a 10-day fair being organized at MMRDA Ground-1, Bandra Kurla Complex from February 16-25, 2023 by the Department of Empowerment of Persons with Disabilities (Divyangjan).

- India's first indigenously developed Train Control and Supervision System, the i-ATS (Indigenous-Automatic Train Supervision) deployed on the Delhi Metro. The iATS was installed on the Red Line that runs between Rithala and Shaheed Sthal.

- The world's highest altitude weather station was destroyed due to hurricane-force winds on Mount Everest and a team of scientists and Sherpa have again placed its new version atop Mount Everest.

- Delhi has outlawed the use of bike taxi services, including those offered by well-known applications like Ola, Uber, and Rapido. The Delhi Transport Department issued the order banning the use of bike taxis on the grounds that doing so is against the law. The department ordered the bike taxi business owners to immediately cease operations.

- Jammu and Kashmir, Lieutenant Governor Manoj Sinha inaugurated the 33rd Police-Public Mela at Gulshan Ground, Jammu. LG Manoj Sinha informed that the Police-Public Mela has emerged as a powerful platform for police officers and the public to interact and celebrate the shared heritage. He commended the Jammu and Kashmir Police Wives Welfare Association (JKPWWA) for carrying out numerous initiatives around the year to address the concerns of the families of martyrs and serving personnel.

- Delhi Metro Rail Corporation will soon launch India's first virtual shopping app called Momentum 2.0 for metro commuters to purchase products, book services and collect orders at the destination stations. The Delhi Metro Rail Corporation has revealed that the app will also provide features such as instant recharge of metro smart cards and smart payment options for other utility services.

- A new type of wheat has been developed by the Indian Council of Agricultural Research (ICAR) to address issues brought on by changing weather patterns and rising temperatures. This brand-new HD-3385 wheat variety may be sown early, evades the effects of heat waves, and is ready for harvest by the end of March.

- In Jammu and Kashmir, 5.9 million tonnes of lithium reserves have been discovered for the first time in India, according to the Mines Ministry's announcement on Thursday (February, 9). According to the Ministry of Mines, the Geological

Survey of India has for the first time discovered 5.9 million tonnes of lithium inferred resources (G3) in the Salal-Haimana area of the Reasi district of Jammu and Kashmir.

- India's top oil firm IOC will set up green hydrogen plants at all its refineries as it pivots a Rs 2-lakh crore green transition plan to achieve net-zero emissions from its operations by 2046, its chairman Shrikant Madhav Vaidya said.

- The Supreme Court of India declined to consider a PIL requesting menstruation leave for workers and students nationwide, citing the issue as one of policy. It was emphasised that menstrual pain leave had various "dimensions" and that, despite the fact that menstruation was a biological event, such leave could discourage businesses from hiring female staff. Only a few nations, mostly in Asia, allow women who experience painful periods to take time off work to heal.

- Sant Sevalal Maharaj, a spiritual and religious figurehead of the Banjara community, was born 284 years ago on February 26, marking the beginning of a yearlong remembrance. Amit Shah, the Union Home Minister, and Meenakshi Lekhi, the Union Minister of State for Foreign Affairs and Culture, led the festivities in New Delhi.

Obituaries

- Former Union law minister and eminent jurist Shanti Bhushan, passed away at the age of 97. He served as the law minister in the Morarji Desai-led Janata Party government from 1977 to 1979, which came to power after Emergency. Bhushan was among the founding members of the Aam Aadmi Party which was formed in 2012. He had also actively participated in the agitation led by social activist Anna Hazare.

- Noted Kannada writer K.V. Tirumalesh, 82, passed away in Hyderabad. K.V. Tirumalesh was suffering from age-related illnesses. He was regarded as one of the most versatile writers across genres and a man with eclectic interests. He is primarily recognized as a poet and honored with the Sahitya Akademi award for his innovative work Akshaya Kavya.

- "a long narrative sans story or aim" as he described it - he wrote extensively across genres, including plays, short stories, novels, translations, and criticism.

- Legendary film director K. Vishwanath passed away in Hyderabad on February 2, at the age of 92 while undergoing treatment for age-related illnesses at a hospital. In a career spanning seven decades, Vishwanath wrote, directed and acted in several movies. Though his work was primarily in Telugu cinema, he also directed several Hindi remakes.

- Pakistan's former president Pervez Musharraf passed away in Dubai at the age of 79 due to a prolonged illness. Musharraf, who was admitted to a hospital in Dubai, was shifted to the Armed Forces Institute of Cardiology (AFIC) in Rawalpindi earlier.

- Vani Jayaram, 78, a legendary playback singer from the South film industry passed away. She breathed her last at her Chennai home in Haddows Road, Nungambakkam. The National Awardee recipient died due to age-related issues. On this year's Republic Day, she was awarded the prestigious Padma Bhushan to recognize her contribution to Indian music for over 50 years.

- Popular artist B.K.S. Verma, has passed away in the city. The subject of his paintings was mainly environmental and social issues presented in a surreal form.

- Italian Skier Elena Fanchini passed at the age of 37 after a toiling battle with cancer on 9th February 2023. Elena Fanchini competed at three Winter Olympics and six World Championships for Italy, and she won a silver medal in the download at the 2005 World Championships. Her last race was in December 2017 after that she stepped away from the game due to her diagnosis.

- Legendary American pop songwriter Burt Bacharach, whose prodigious work created a chart-topping soundtrack for the 1960s and 1970s, passed away at the age of 94.

- Veteran theatre and film actor Javed Khan Amrohi, best known for his roles in the popular DD serial Nukkad and films such as Lagaan and Chak De! India, passed away at the age of 70s. After graduating from the Film and Television Institute of

India (FTII), Amrohi appeared in smaller yet pivotal roles in over 150 films and close to a dozen TV shows.

- Eminent Indian painter and late filmmaker Guru Dutt's sister Lalitha Lajmi passed away at the age of 90. She was born to a poet father and a poly-linguistic writer mother in Kolkata in 1932. She was a self-taught artist with a keen interest in classical dance.

- Tulsidas Balaram, one of the country's finest footballers and a member of the golden era of Indian football (1951-1962), passed away. He was 86. He played in two Olympics in 1956 and 1960 and reached the pinnacle of Asian football when India, under the guidance of legendary coach Syed Abdul Rahim, won the Asian Games gold in Jakarta, beating South Korea 2-1 in 1962. Balaram scored 131 goals, including 14 for India, across seven seasons.

- Shahnawaz Pradhan, best known for featuring in series Mirzapur and movie Raees, has passed away. He was in his late 50s. He has played character roles in films M.S Dhoni: The Untold Story, Khuda Haafiz, Raees and Phantom; web series The Family Man and Hostages, and TV show Krishna and 24 among others.

- Famous Yakshagana singer and screenwriter Balipa Narayan Bhagwat passed away at the age of 85 . He had mastered a unique style of singing, due to which fans have given it the name of 'Balipa Style'. Rich in voice, Bhagwat has written more than 30 Yakshagana 'Prasanga' (scripts).

- Telugu actor and politician Nandamuri Taraka Ratna has passed away at the age of 39 due to cardiac arrest. Taraka Ratna was the grandson of legendary film actor and former Andhra Pradesh Chief Minister late NT Rama Rao and son of Nandamuri Mohan Krishna.

- Former Gujarat governor and veteran Bharatiya Janata Party (BJP) leader Om Prakash Kohli has passed away at the age of 87. He was the 19th governor of Gujarat from 2014 to 2019. While presiding as Gujarat governor, he also served as the governor of Madya Pradesh and Goa. A former Rajya Sabha member and ex-president of BJP in Delhi, he was also a leading academician.

- Subi Suresh, a 41-year-old actor and television host from Malayalam, passed dead. The actor's first theatre roles were as a comic and dancer.
- Classical dance legend Kanak Rele passed away at the age of 85. The Mohiniyattam exponent, who was awarded the first Guru Gopinath National Puraskaram of the Government of Kerala.

www.ingramcontent.com/pod-product-compliance
Ingram Content Group UK Ltd.
Pitfield, Milton Keynes, MK11 3LW, UK
UKHW061704190726
13853UKWH00008B/2400

9 789355 566522